FROM THE GROUND UP

A PARABLE FOR CULTIVATING A MISSIONAL CHURCH

DWIGHT M. GUNTER II

f

THE FOUNDRY
PUBLISHING

Copyright © 2025 by Dwight M. Gunter II
The Foundry Publishing®
PO Box 419527
Kansas City, MO 64141
thefoundrypublishing.com

978-0-8341-4318-0

Printed in the
United States of America

Cover design: Caines Design
Interior design: Sharon Page

Library of Congress Cataloging-in-Publication Data
A complete catalog record for this book is available from the Library of Congress.

10 9 8 7 6 5 4 3 2 1

CONTENTS

■──────■

INTRODUCTION

■————■

Information overload is pandemic. Distractions in our lives are infinite. These demagogues often prevent us from focusing on the real mission given to us as followers of Christ. Yet we do have a mission! Christ himself gave us *his* mission and commissioned us to fulfill it in this world by the empowerment of the Holy Spirit. Yet we are too often defeated by information overload and distraction.

Add to these complications the reality that leading a church is more of an art than a science. In fact, it is much like a dance. Dances have steps and moves and require cooperation and teamwork as well as timing, rhythm, and synchrony, but it would be preposterous to reduce dancing to a series of properly ordered steps. It is an art. Leading churches involves many steps, and it definitely requires cooperation and teamwork as well as timing, rhythm, and synchrony. But make no mistake, it is an art filled with chemistry and passion. As such, it takes time, space, and place to create. Distractions, diversions, tyrannical urgencies, and the agendas of other people or organizations often impede us as we attempt the awesome art of leading a church.

Can we overcome these obstacles? Can the Holy Spirit truly empower the church—the followers of Jesus—to be missionally effective in a world that seems to be filled with emptiness while devolving into chaos?

I have hope! And my hope is not based on the past record of the church but rather on the faithfulness of the triune God. God the Father, Son, and Holy Spirit is active in our world today and deeply desires the church to join in the *missio Dei*. Here's what I know:

- God deeply desires the restoration of all creation.
- The Father will not let the Christ event be wasted.
- Jesus will build his church and advance his kingdom.
- The same Holy Spirit who filled the church at Pentecost still fills and empowers the followers of Jesus today.
- Our faithfulness to Christ and to the *missio Dei* is our Holy Spirit-empowered responsibility (results are up to God, who gives the increase).

This project is specifically intended for church leaders, whether lay or clergy. It is also for anyone who cares about the church and longs for the church to be an effective partner with God in his mission in the world. My deep desire is for this book to come alongside you and assist you in your journey, helping you to be missionally effective as we who name the name of Jesus join him in restoring the world and setting it right.

Please note that even though this book does not address planting churches, it is firmly in the mind of the author that healthy churches plant churches. If a local church truly gets healthy, it will plant new churches or expressions of churches. This book is intended to help congregations move toward functional health.

My prayer for the church is for God to renew our focus on Christ, to enlighten us with wisdom, and to empower us for *God's* mission. Our world desperately needs a church who is fully committed to Jesus and completely engaged in God's mission. With the apostle Paul, I pray

that the God of our Lord Jesus Christ, the Father of glory, may give you a spirit of wisdom and revelation as you come to know him, so that, with the eyes of your heart enlightened, you may perceive what is the hope to which he has called you, what are the riches of his glorious inheritance among the saints, and what is the immeasurable greatness of his power for us who believe, according to the working of his great power. God put this power to work in Christ when he raised him from the dead and seated him at his right hand in the heavenly places, far above all rule and authority and power and dominion and above every name that is named, not only in this age but also in the age to come. And he has put all things under his feet and has made him the head over all things for the church, which is his body, the fullness of him who fills all in all. (Ephesians 1:17–23)

1

HOW DID I GET HERE?

Daniel sat in his office staring out the window. His mind was churning around so many issues he couldn't focus on any one of them. He needed to write his sermon, but for some reason he couldn't get motivated. Questions, stress, diverted vision . . . he felt like he was trying to run in wet concrete.

Why is our church not growing? Why do we seem to be shrinking—or stagnant, at best? I thought for sure the new program would work! Doesn't every church experience some growth from a social media blitz? Why do other churches seem to take off but ours doesn't?

COVID-19 didn't help matters at all! It felt like people were looking for an excuse to stay away from church. "Why attend when we can just watch from home?" He'd heard that enough to be sick of the question. It wasn't difficult to see the connection between this question and the consumeristic, entertainment orientation of the broader culture.

The pandemic had wreaked havoc in the church in more ways than one. The political polarization it highlighted and exacerbated was dizzying. Mask, no masks! Vaccines, no vaccines! CDC guidelines or forget the government! There simply could be no consensus in many people's minds. Plus, resurfacing racial tensions created so much suspicion and distrust that the work of the kingdom felt impotent. Daniel mused, "Perhaps the gates of hell are prevailing after all."

All these issues simply added to his long list of questions. He took very little solace from the reality that everyone was dealing with the same things, and his questions never seemed to loiter far from the front of his mind:

- Why is our church not growing?
- Why do we seem to be shrinking—or stagnant, at best?
- Why do other churches take off but ours doesn't?
- Why is church so *hard* these days?

Daniel Grant had been a pastor for seventeen years at three different churches. His first two charges had followed the traditions of their denomination. They were good churches but were both reluctant to take risks in order to attract more people. They had experienced small growth at best, but they consoled themselves by believing they were doing better than most other churches, especially in their denomination.

Yet Pastor Daniel wanted more. He had entered pastoral ministry because of a divine call on his life. Being a pastor was God's plan for his life, and God had gifted and graced him to join his mission in this fashion. As a result, Daniel wanted to do something great for God.

Calvary had been a great place to start. The small congregation of blue-collar folks gave him room to learn. He certainly made his share of mistakes, but they had offered him grace and loved him anyway. "Just don't change too many things around here and everything will be okay" had been their repeated mantra to Pastor Daniel. And they were right. Things *were* okay. But Pastor Daniel wanted more than just *okay,* so when the opportunity came for him to go to First Church in a larger, more populated area, Daniel knew it was the will of God. He took his wife, Erin, and their daughter, Caroline, and set out for the new land. Surely this would be the place where he could try some of his new ideas and implement some of the programs he'd heard about at a recent church leadership conference.

Instead, he encountered more of the same, just on a slightly larger scale. Pastor Daniel found that a larger congregation in a larger town didn't automatically translate to a more progressive church. In fact, what he found was that, in this case anyway, more people simply resulted in more problems, more resistance to change, more impediments to doing something great for God. He discovered that bigger doesn't equal better. They were two different concepts. Bigger is bigger, and better is better. They are not synonyms.

Disillusionment set in after five years, and Daniel prayed that God would send him somewhere else—anywhere else—to a place that would take a chance and at least try to do things differently. Daniel then left his second pastorate to become the pastor of Grace Community Church. Before Daniel accepted the position of lead pastor, he met with the church leadership team, who had quite a few questions for him.

- What is your leadership style?
- What is your vision for the church?
- Do you preach or do you teach?
- What style of music do you prefer?
- Who will be your main target audience—the younger generations, or the older folks who pay the bills?

Pastor Daniel knew the last two questions were land mines, but he had walked through this minefield before. He was relieved when his answers matched the expectations of the church leadership. They seemed to breathe a sigh of relief as well, and all appeared to be a good fit between Daniel and the congregation.

Erin liked the church too, and felt it was time to leave their second pastorate. Her excitement level over the possibilities in ministry matched Daniel's. Plus, the church didn't seem to have any predetermined plans for her as the pastor's wife. They simply wanted her to find a place of ministry and do the things God had gifted her to do. It was refreshing, and Erin was excited! They loaded up Caroline and their second child, Charlie, and set out for the promised land.

Four years later, Pastor Daniel found himself asking the same questions he'd asked in his previous churches: *Why is our church not growing? Why do we seem to be shrinking—or stagnant, at best? Growth is happening other churches—why not here?*

When Pastor Daniel had arrived at Grace Community, he immediately began to implement his new programs and ideas. The people were receptive, and he didn't meet the usual resistance to change that he'd encountered at his previous pastorates. He honestly believed this was *it*—whatever *it* is. This was the place and these were the people who would follow his lead. Now they could get somewhere. Now they could do something great for God. Yet, a mere four years later he was seeing the early weeds of disappointment peeking through the mulch of the programs he'd initiated.

"I have to get away and think," Daniel told Erin.

"I need some time to pray and meditate on our next steps," he informed his church leadership.

So Daniel planned his trip to the vacation mountain home of one of his parishioners. If he could just get away from everything and everyone and get alone with God, surely God would give him wisdom. Somehow Daniel knew this was going to be a monumental time for him. He packed his bags, gathered the books he wanted, picked up his computer and iPad, and got an early start, heading off to the hills to hear from God.

The two-hundred-mile trip to the mountain home was filled with more questions than mile markers. The farther he traveled, the more lost Daniel felt.

- Had he missed the will of God so long ago when he believed God called him to the ministry?
- Had he misunderstood God's direction when he changed pastorates?
- Should he get out of the role of lead pastor and join a staff somewhere? He had made many good friends of fellow pastors; surely one of them needed help on their staff.
- Are there other programs he should try that would be more effective?
- Was he doing something wrong?
- Was he missing something obvious?
- Was he no longer effective as a leader?
- Did God want him to be a pastor only for the first part of his life?

How did I get here? Where should I go next? These questions and many others bombarded Daniel's spirit in rapid-fire, leaving him even more disenchanted with the whole idea of being a pastor. Without question, he needed answers! He didn't want to live his life without making a difference in the world. Somehow this time with God was going to be a watershed experience. He just knew it!

When Daniel arrived at the mountain home, it was better than expected. It was beautiful! And the setting—wow! He found the home in a little secluded valley surrounded by seven mountain peaks. The refreshing stream at the base of the back porch was so clear he felt like drinking from it. The stream immediately became a symbol of the refreshing for which his soul so desperately longed. He could imagine his time at this place being invigorating, sitting on the back porch and thinking, meditating, reading, praying, analyzing, contemplating. If the weather would cooperate—and how could it not in such a perfect place?—this was going to be a time he would never forget.

Little did Daniel know how right he was.

Daniel's downhearted spirit seemed to perk up, and his glaring disillusionment hinted at fading just by arriving at this beautiful place. It was as if this spot of earth opened his ears to the Creator God, who was saying, *"I'm here and I'm ready to meet with you."* Was this like one of those Celtic Christian "thin places" Daniel had heard about?

He quickly unpacked his suitcase, emptied his bags of groceries into the refrigerator and cabinets, and put on a pot of coffee. The Costa Rican organic coffee was his favorite, and he had brought three bags for this week. With a cup of coffee in one hand and his Bible in the other, Daniel pulled up a chair at the little patio table on the back porch. "Okay God," he said. "I'm ready. Show me. Teach me. I'm all eyes and ears."

Daniel began his prayer time with Psalm 150, followed by the Doxology and an invocation. He wanted to start with praise, and he felt he needed to ask God to work in his life, so Daniel prayed a prayer from the *Book of Common Prayer* that he'd grown to love: *Almighty God, unto whom all hearts are open, all desires known, and from whom no secrets are hid: Cleanse the thoughts of our hearts by the inspiration of the Holy Spirit, that we may perfectly love you, and worthily magnify your holy name; through Christ our Lord. Amen.* Daniel continued to pray as inspired by James 4:7–8: *God, I submit myself to you, and I resist the forces of evil in the name of Jesus. Help me by YOUR Holy Spirit to draw close to you.* He added Psalm 139:23–24 (NIV) to his prayer: *"Search me, God, and know my heart; test me and know my anxious thoughts. See if there is any offensive way in me, and lead me in the way everlasting."*

With his attention in the right place and his heart open to the Holy Spirit, Daniel prayed and tried his best to listen to the impressions of God on his heart. He was convinced that nothing good—certainly nothing of eternal value—ever happened without prayer. In fact, he knew he could do a lot of things *after* prayer but nothing of real value *before* prayer. Surely, in this place, in this setting, and at this time, God would speak, and Daniel would be able to hear.

2

SOMETHING HAS TO CHANGE!

As Daniel sat at the patio table on the back porch, his attention turned from the sound of the babbling creek to the sight of the surrounding peaks. As his eyes scanned the panoramic view, one specific peak caught his eye. Was there movement on the hilltop, or was it just his imagination? The more he stared the more certain he was—he did indeed see something. There it was again—smoke. In this secluded place? He needed to take a look. There might be a problem that needed investigating.

Daniel left the comfortable chair on the back porch and found a trail across the valley floor to the base of the peak where he'd seen the smoke. He was now totally convinced there was a problem because the smoke was obvious. But how could he climb the hillside to get to the place from where the smoke emanated? His eye fell across a game trail, a footpath used by the creatures of the valley. Up the trail he went until he found the source of the smoke, where he found a scene he had not expected.

There, seated on a log, was an older man with long, white, wavy hair. Daniel smiled as he thought about how much the man resembled the old preachers of the nineteenth century. He'd seen their pictures and read their stories during seminary days. Here sat a man who looked just like them—white wavy hair, goatee with a handlebar mustache, blue jeans, and a frock coat.

The man addressed Daniel. "Sit down, young man. Have a seat. There's plenty of room on the log."

"Thanks," Daniel said, and sat. Then he asked the man, "Who are you, and what are you doing here?" The strangeness of the scene let Daniel feel free to be direct.

The old man said, "My name is Samuel Cooper Stewart; my friends call me Sam. Feel free to be my friend. I was about to ask you the same question. Who are you, and what are you doing here?"

Daniel offered an abbreviated version of who he was, what he did for a living, and said he was there on a personal retreat of sorts.

Sam turned toward Daniel, looked him directly in the eye, and said, "I already knew your story, but you still haven't answered my question: Who are *you* and what are *you* doing here?"

For a moment Daniel didn't exactly know how to respond. It was a good question. In fact, it was the root question that had set him on this quest in the first place. *Who am I, and what am I doing here?*

"You know, Sam, I could have answered that question ten years ago. I could have even answered it four years ago. Today, I'm not really sure. In fact, I feel at times I'm not sure about much. For over a year now I've been asking—or

17

trying not to ask—that very question. Who am I, and what am I doing here?"

"Hmm!" Sam grunted. "That's interesting. Found any answers yet?"

"Not really," Daniel said before he even thought. "But at least I'm taking some steps to ask it honestly."

"Hmm!" Sam grunted again, but this time as if he were deep in thought. "Daniel, you ever think that maybe you're asking a *good* question but not the *first* question?"

"What do you mean?" Daniel was puzzled.

"Well, what is the center of your world? Maybe, better phrased, *who* is the center of your world? Or, whose world is it anyway?" Sam was deeper than he appeared, and Daniel began to see him as more than just an itinerant preacher— he was more like a nineteenth-century naturalist philosopher. "Do you think the Creator God who spoke the worlds into existence *needs* you to do something great *for* him?"

"Ah! I see where you're going with this. I've been thinking *I* have to do something *for* God—as if it's all about *me* and what *I* am to do in *my* world. Even in trying to do it *for* God it was still all about *me*—my accomplishments, abilities, gifts, achievements, goals, and plans."

"Think about it, Daniel. What can *you* really do for *God*? What does God *need*? Did you honestly think that in the end, when you stand before God, you would stand beside a stack of accomplishments and impress God with all the glorious goals you achieved *for* him?"

"Well . . . I wouldn't have said it exactly like that, but in practice I guess that is exactly the way I've been living." There was a long pause that bordered on awkward while Sam wisely let Daniel internalize his thoughts.

"I'm embarrassed! How could I, a minister of the gospel, fall into the trap of thinking I could do anything worthwhile *for* God?" There was a glimmer of light in Daniel's mind now.

Sam returned to his sermon. "Don't you know, haven't you heard, didn't you read in the Bible where Jesus said to his disciples, 'If any wish to come after me, let them deny themselves and take up their cross and follow me'"? (Matthew 16:24). "Or what about Paul? He had a list of accomplishments a mile long. If anyone could have done anything great *for* God, it would have been Paul. But even Paul said, 'Yet whatever gains I had, these I have come to regard as loss because of Christ'" (Philippians 3:7). "If that is not enough—" Sam took a deep breath, caught his stride, and kept preaching— "God called Abram to leave all, not knowing where he was going, how it would turn out, or what God even had in mind. But Abram understood he couldn't stay where he was and still pursue God, so he left the familiar and followed God."

Sam paused in dramatic fashion to let those words sink into the soil of Daniel's soul. After a moment, Daniel broke the silence. "Paul was right: some plant, others water, but God gives the increase" (see 1 Corinthians 3:6).

"Daniel, you're starting to see it. But think of that passage again. Paul specifically said, 'I planted, Apollos watered, but *God* gave the growth. So neither the one who plants nor the one who waters is anything, but *only God* who gives the growth. The one who plants and the one who waters have one purpose, and each will receive wages according to their own labor. For we are God's co-workers, working together; you are God's field, God's building'" (1 Corinthians 3:6–9). "Paul's perspective was that it is all about *God*, what *he's* doing, where *he's* doing it, and how *he's* doing it. We are to work, for sure, but it is *God*-centered. To use the theological term, it is Christo-centric. It's all about Christ. We are *followers* of Christ before we are *doers.*"

Sam wasn't through. "We aren't anything apart from God. Our value, our worth, any sense of mission and meaning in life, all comes from our relationship with Christ. It flows from our *following* him. It really is *all* about Jesus! Therefore—" Sam was zooming in on his point like a great orator— "maybe the first question is not: Who are you, and what are you doing here? Maybe the first question is: Who is *God*, and what is *he* doing here?"

Again there was a dramatic pause. Sam was a good preacher, and Daniel felt like he needed to respond in some way. "Sam, you're talking about the consumer mentality that has permeated the heart of the church—that perspective of self-centeredness that causes us to view everything by how it affects *us*—me. I've preached against the consumer mentality for years. I've preached about how self-centeredness is the wellspring of our problems. Adam and Eve acted selfishly in the garden, and therefore sin entered the world. We have been struggling with self-absorption ever since. I've talked about how self-obsession is like wearing contacts—how, after a while, you forget you even have them on. You just see things differently. What I didn't realize was that I had fallen into the same trap. I forgot that the calling was to follow Jesus. The calling is to *come and follow* more so than *go and do*. And if I don't come and follow, my going and doing will amount to failure."

Daniel sat back down, not having realized he had gotten up from the log and begun to pace. The openness, honesty, and authenticity before God were beginning to refresh his soul. It was like taking that first drink of cool, clear water before you had your fill.

Sam pointed to the fire and asked, "Want a hot dog?" Daniel hadn't even noticed that Sam was roasting hot dogs over the open flame. "I love hot dogs," Sam said. "There's never a bad time to have a hot dog. Too bad I don't have the chili, onions, and slaw out here. Those accoutrements just glorify an old hot dog."

Daniel grabbed a hot dog off the stick where it was simmering over the fire, shoved it in his mouth, and began talking before he even swallowed. His mind raced with the ramifications of his new perspective. "You know, Sam, what is true of me is also true of the church I pastor—and even true of Christianity today in general. *We have forgotten our identity!* Perhaps more to the point, we have forgotten the Creator God! We have forgotten who we are and *whose* we are! We've turned in on ourselves and made church all about us. We debate the worship styles *we* like, the buildings *we* want to build, the times *we* want to meet, the programs *we* want to start, and even the people *we* want to reach—as if God is a divine bellhop, just standing there waiting to give us what *we* want."

Daniel began to see an image from his theology class from years before. He remembered the idea of sin being described as *homo incurvatus in se*—humanity turned in on ourselves. The professor had taught them that one way of describing the sin issue was to talk about how God is the Creator, the Maker of heaven and earth. We are the creatures, formed and given life by the Creator God. We, the creatures, are to worship the Creator. We, the creatures, are to live our lives under the direction—the lordship—of

God. We are to remember that our identity is creature, not creator.

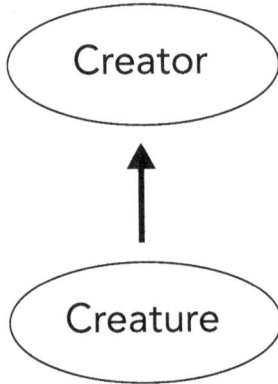

Creator

↑

Creature

However, we have curved in on ourselves, worshiping the creature instead of the Creator—which is sin. That was the first and second of the Ten Commandments—no other gods and no idols. When we make life all about us, it is sin. We lose our identity. Life gets out of sorts. We are not *right*. We miss the mark. We lose our way. Brokenness results.

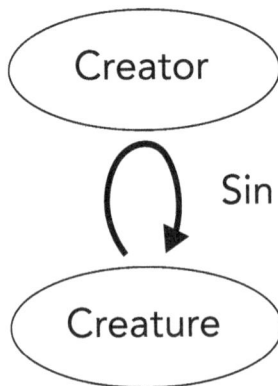

Creator

Sin

Creature

All the images and illustrations Daniel had ever used to describe sin came back to him like a wall of water, washing over his mind and revealing the bare rocks in its wake. It made sense.

Another light illuminated additional thoughts. If that were true of an individual's life—and it was without doubt—couldn't it be true of the church as the body of Christ? Could the church be guilty of turning in on itself, missing the mark, worshiping itself rather than its Head? Is that why there was so much brokenness with the church? Would it be accurate to call that *organizational sin*?

- When churches—communities of Jesus followers— stop following Jesus and expect Jesus to show up at their events and gatherings, they are committing organizational sin.

- When it is all about worship styles rather than worshiping the Savior, it is organizational sin.

- When Christians focus on how to grow in number so they can be more important, rather than how to be used by God to transform the lives of others and even the world itself, it is organizational sin.

- When believers concentrate their efforts and resources on doing something *for* God rather than placing themselves and their resources in the hands of Christ and allowing him to do something *through* them, it is organizational sin.

- When the church aligns itself with secular sources of power, influence, and politics, it is organizational sin.

- When churches want everyone else to experience Jesus just like they have traditionally experienced Jesus, could they be committing organizational sin?

Evidently the church has forgotten its identity and its reason for existence. And, as a leader in the church, Daniel was guilty!

Daniel spoke his ponderings out loud. "No wonder people are leaving the organized church today! No wonder people say they love Jesus but not the church! No wonder many people now outside the church who once were in the church don't want to be associated with the church! No wonder some folks have dismissed the church entirely and labeled it antiquated, giving up on it! No wonder some are speaking with a prophetic voice to the church in hopes of transforming the church! We have committed organizational sin! We have failed to remember that all of life—including church life—is wholly about Jesus. And," Daniel continued, "the place where the church meets—whether a traditional sanctuary, a gymnasium, a storefront, a house, under a tree, at a workplace, in cyberspace—is not as important as *what* the church *is*. We are the body of Christ—the covenant people of God—and as such our lives are to center on him. It is all about the mission of God in this world—his world. It is all about the nature of God being lived out in this world, thereby resulting in the mission of God being accomplished in this world—his world! The first question really is: Who is *God*, and what is *he* doing here?"

Daniel turned to Sam, but Sam was gone—vanished, as if he'd never been there. The only signs remaining were the smoldering embers and the lingering taste of a great hot dog.

The sun was setting, and the sky gave a beautiful glow of orange fading into various shades of purple. There was a wonderful coolness in the air as Daniel made his way back to the house. As he thought about his conversation with Sam, he felt a deep peace. He knew he hadn't solved his issues, and he still had countless questions to ask and answer, but he felt like he was on the right track.

Once he had eaten supper and washed the dishes, Daniel walked out on the back porch to breathe in the cool night air. He was hoping Sam might show up, but somehow he intuitively knew Sam wasn't coming around that night. As Daniel listened to the sounds of the night, replete with crickets, he was lost in thought. "Jesus, please forgive me for thinking it was all about me. I open my mind and heart to you. Teach me. Give me wisdom to understand your ways and your heart."

3

THE FOUNDATIONS

Morning was spectacular. Daniel woke early, in time to walk out on the front porch and watch the sunrise. He felt that the sunrise was symbolic of this trip and of the light that was beginning to dawn in him. Maybe it would be bright enough before he left.

As Daniel looked out over the hillsides that stood like sentinels on each side of the road leading to the mountain home, his eye focused on a red-tailed hawk. Hawks are such majestic birds, and he wanted a closer look at the soaring creature. Grabbing his binoculars, he watched the bird glide across the blue sky and swoop down on its breakfast for the day.

Just then, something bright appeared in the corner of his eye. *What was that?* Daniel wondered. Unable to find it in the binoculars, he put them down. There it was again—like sunlight reflecting off glass. *Time for another hike*, Daniel thought.

With his water bottle and an energy bar in hand, Daniel started out in the direction of the reflection.

He climbed the slope and entered a clearing about halfway up the mountain. Walking became a little easier as he relaxed on the rather wide path he'd found.

Suddenly, he tripped. "What in the world?" he said out loud as he looked up at the sky. Flat on his back from the unexpected fall, he heard a voice respond to his bewildered inquiry.

"Oh, that's an old railroad spike. I thought they had picked up all of those when this line went away, but I guess they missed one. Easy to do—there were so many."

Startled, Daniel jumped to his feet. "Who are you?"

"My name is Ed Griggs. I walk on this old railroad bed quite often. I'm fascinated that, after all this time, the foundation for the rail remains. It was built so long ago— this section in the summer of 1855 if I recall. Man, was it hot that summer! Humid too! We worked virtually nonstop to get this portion completed before the winter snows set in. The investors wanted us to hurry it along. People were tired of being isolated. 'Cut corners anywhere you can,' they said. 'Get it done. Time is money.' They kept after us, but we knew something they tended to overlook. In fact, most people trying to get there in a hurry overlook it."

Daniel thought he was awake. He thought he'd had his coffee. He thought he had taken a walk. But it all now seemed like a Twilight Zone experience. He decided he had to just go with it. After all, he'd just spent the previous day with Sam, a different complete stranger in this wilderness where he'd come for a retreat.

"Okay," Daniel said, knowing Ed had intended for him to ask. "What did they overlook?"

"Why, the foundation, of course. You see, son, the foundation is key. Without the right foundation, everything that follows is tenuous at best. It runs the risk of eroding and collapsing when encountering any degree of adversity. If it's a building, just let the wind blow a little stronger than usual and great will be the fall thereof. In the case of the railroad, a little too much rain or snow meeting an unstable foundation, and—catastrophe! The financial ramifications are nothing compared to the loss of life. Foundations are, well, foundational!"

"How do you know so much about this?" It all made sense to Daniel, but how did this guy know?

"I'm the engineer who designed this railroad. I laid out this section. It was a little tricky when we got to the pass, and it took us a while to get a solid-enough base in place to lay the rails. But they never had an erosion problem. The foundation stayed strong through it all—the rockslides, torrential rains, hard winter snows, you name it. This track was solid. The people who got on board could trust it. It wasn't going anywhere. Well, son, I've been talking the whole time about this railroad bed. I can't get over my admiration for it. But tell me, what brings you out here in the middle of the mountains?"

Daniel began to tell his story and why he had come to the mountain home. "I'm just trying to find some direction and figure out what's going on, where I need go, or what I should do."

"Sounds like your train has run off the tracks. Or, maybe, your tracks have broken away because your foundations weren't built properly. Tell me, Daniel, what is the foundation to *your* train? What is the bedrock of *your* ministry?"

"Good question, Ed. My first response is all the programs we operate. We have ministries to children, youth, and various adult ages. We have programs to help people in need and in crisis. Those things have become foundational to us."

"Really?" Ed didn't seem convinced. "They sound more like train cars to me. What are the *programs*, as you call them, based on? What gives substance to the programs? Where do your leaders get direction for those programs? You have to look deeper, son, to find the foundations."

"I haven't thought of it that way. Wow!" Daniel paused in reflection while Ed let him think.

Daniel finally offered an answer. "Maybe the foundation, the bedrock on which the church is built, is the Word of God."

"I'm an engineer and not a theologian, but I've taught my share of Sunday school classes. Do you mean the written Word or the living Word?"

Daniel responded, "I think I mean Jesus Christ. And, of course, the Bible tells his story. Jesus is the living Word who said to Peter, 'And I tell you, you are Peter, and on this rock I will build my church, and the gates of Hades will not prevail against it'" (Matthew 16:18).

"I have to say it is the living Word," Daniel continued, "but I also have to say it is the written Word. Paul said to Timothy, 'All Scripture is inspired by God and is useful for teaching, for reproof, for correction, and for training in righteousness, so that the person of God may be proficient, equipped for every good work'" (2 Timothy 3:16–17).

"In other words, Daniel, it's both. You encounter the living Word through the written Word. What you know about Jesus, you learn through the written Word. And through the written Word, you experience the living Word. Sound right?"

"Your point is well made, Ed. The Word of God—the living Word *and* that which conveys the authority of the living Word—is the foundation for all ministry."

Ed wasn't finished probing, "Wouldn't a follower of Jesus say that the Word of God is really the foundation for all of life? Are we not to let the Spirit of God through the Word of God teach us, shape us, direct us, and transform us into whatever God intends? And why would you think the church—the body of Christ—is any different than you as an individual? If our lives individually are to be shaped by the Spirit through the Word, don't you think our lives corporately should be shaped by the Spirit through the Word? If the foundation of your life individually is the Word, shouldn't you begin to think of the church's life as being grounded on the Word?"

"Are you sure you're not a theologian, Ed? That's great thinking!"

"Not a trained one, anyway, but I do know a bit about foundations, and I know that any endeavor, any organization, any organism must have a good and sure foundation. And I know there's no surer foundation than the Word of God. In fact, if I recall, God said through Isaiah the prophet, 'See, I am laying in Zion a foundation stone, a tested stone, a precious cornerstone, a sure foundation: One who trusts will not panic'" (Isaiah 28:16). Ed's mind turned to the New Testament. "Jesus said the same thing. He taught foundations to the people. He said, 'Everyone, then, who hears these words of mine and acts on them will be like a wise man who built his house on rock. The rain fell, the floods came, and the winds blew and beat on that house, but it did not fall because it had been founded on rock. And everyone who hears these words of mine and does not act on them will be like a foolish man who built his house on sand. The rain fell, and the floods came, and the winds blew and beat against that house, and it fell—and great was its fall!'" (Matthew 7:24–27).

Ed continued, "Do you remember what happened after Jesus told that story, son? Matthew said, 'Now when Jesus had finished saying these words, the crowds were astounded at his teaching, for he taught them as one having authority and not as their scribes'" (Matthew 7:28–29). "Authority. Foundations. They are connected. The proper foundation will give you the authority to build your structure. The foundations are key!"

Daniel jumped in, "God is the Authority, and the Word of God is the foundation on which we can create programs, ministries, goals, and objectives. You've given me something to think about, Ed."

"Well, son, I think I'll just mosey on down this railroad bed. I do enjoy walking through this foundation. I learn something new every time I take this stroll. I'll be seeing you."

With that, Ed disappeared around the bend, but his words did not. Daniel had something to think about for a while.

As Daniel climbed up to the top of the hill he looked back down and could see the ribbon of railroad bed as it wound its way around the curves of the mountains. It had been there for so long. Countless numbers of people had staked their lives on it. No one could name all the people who trusted it on their journeys in life. *How true that is of the Word!* Daniel thought with joy. *Counting the people who have staked their very lives on the Word and trusted the Word on their journey through life would be like . . . like counting the sands on the seashore or the stars in the heavens. The right foundation gives life to all who build on it.* "I have to get into the Word today," Daniel said out loud to himself.

With that plan for the afternoon, Daniel walked back to the house, got his Bible, and began to dig in, letting both the written and the living Word excavate his soul. Sitting on the porch, Bible in hand, Daniel began to grapple with the heart of the foundation: the Word of God, written and living. There must be an affirmation of a foundation!

Daniel prayed, "Jesus, your brother James said that if anyone lacked wisdom to ask you for it and you would give it. I need wisdom to understand this foundational issue."

As Daniel kept praying and grappling with the issue, the light appeared in his mind. "I'm reading the Word of God, talking to the Son of God, empowered by the Spirit of God. Jesus is the foundation. The triune God—Father, Son, and Holy Spirit—is the foundation. The nature of God as revealed in the Word of God is the heart of the foundation. The Bible is foundational only because it reveals the authoritative triune God. Why haven't I seen that before?" The light of the noonday sun seemed dim compared to the light shining in his mind: everything we do must be based on—grounded in—the Word. Everything! The Word is the foundation!

Daniel spent the rest of the day thinking about the ramifications of that truth. He remembered reading the book *Purpose-Driven Church,* by Rick Warren, and how Warren had discovered the various driving forces of churches and ministries: tradition, personality, finances, programs, buildings, events, seekers, or fads. If the foundation were the Word, the church would be protected from being dominated by these forces. We cannot afford to be in contradiction to the Word regarding how we do church. If we are, the foundations will not be stable, lives will be lost, and people will not reach their destination.

Unexpectedly, Daniel didn't sleep well that night. His mind churned with the events of the day. His spirit grappled with the implications of the Word as foundational. The restless night gave way to a gray morning as rain echoed off the tin roof.

4

AN OLD FRIEND

"I need to get up," Daniel said aloud to himself. "But lying here in this comfortable bed on this rainy morning after a restless night is just too tempting." Nevertheless, Daniel crawled out of bed and splashed water in his eyes to wake himself up. Then he walked out on the back porch and took a seat in one of the rocking chairs. The rain continued, and the air had a tinge of chill in it. The slight breeze magnified the coolness. *I need a sweatshirt this morning*, he thought. *I'll get it in a minute.* Leaning his head against the back of the rocking chair, Daniel continued his thoughts from the day and night before. The nature of God, the essence of who he is, the Word—living and written—is foundational. But what does that look like in everyday practice?

Sam had helped him see that the focus must be on God and his work in the world. It was all about God, not about Daniel, the church leadership, or anyone's plans or desires. It was all about God. Everything was to focus on him.

Ed helped him understand that the foundation for living in general and for doing the work of the church was the Word of God. The essential nature of the triune God is somehow particularly integral to the foundation. Daniel was determined to figure this out.

Daniel was becoming aware of sounds in the background, like pots and pans banging around along with coffee grinding. *Who on earth would be rummaging around in the house? There's no one around for miles.*

When Daniel stepped inside the screen door that led straight into the kitchen, he had to do a double take. There at the sink with two coffee cups in her hands stood one of his favorite people in the world—his old theology professor. Dr. Anne Darden was known as one of the toughest professors in the history of Aldersgate College, the small liberal arts school Daniel had called home for four great years. Her tests were infamous. Would-be theologians studied for days and wrote for hours to complete one of her three-question tests. She graded very strictly. In fact, she could be severe. Daniel sat next to a student who was awarded a 7 on a 100-point test. As tough as her reputation was, Daniel knew from their after-class chats that she cared about her students beyond measure. In fact, the reason she held them to such high standards of accountability was that she loved them so much. She believed in each student and in the God who had called them.

But in this moment, seeing Dr. Darden standing there was very uncomfortable. The 7 his friend received was at least twice as high as the grade Daniel thought he'd get if she knew just how he was struggling in ministry these days. What mysterious force had brought her to this kitchen? She had been with the Lord for about three years. Given the strangeness of Sam and Ed, Daniel took it in stride and asked, "Dr. Darden? What brings you here?"

"You do, Daniel. Here, have a cup of coffee. It's just what the doctor ordered for a rainy day and restless mind. I hope you don't mind, but I took the liberty of building a fire in the family room. It's a little chilly today."

They stepped into the family room where there was a nice, cozy fire burning beautifully. One thing Daniel loved about this house was all the rocking chairs. They each chose one and sat down comfortably. The entire scene looked like a picture from the *Southern Living* magazine—fireplace, coffee, rocking chairs, and rain falling on a tin roof. The atmosphere was flawless for great conversation.

"Talk to me, Daniel. Where are you struggling? What are you thinking?"

Daniel recapped the struggles he had encountered as a pastor. He thought that in the right place he could initiate his programmatic ideas and success would be sure to follow. He told her of his conversation with Sam that led to his confession of self-centeredness. He relayed the meeting with Ed and how it led him to deeper questions about the nature of God.

"You're on the right path, Daniel. We must come to the end of ourselves in order for God to work through us as effectively as he desires. So many Christians in general, and pastors in particular, are working *for* God, but they are making the decisions and plans themselves. It is about their kingdom rather than God's kingdom. And really, you could say they make it about their *empire* instead of God's *kingdom*. There is a difference."

Dr. Darden continued, "So many followers of Christ let themselves get in the way of what God wants to do in the world. They mean well. They care about Jesus and people, but they just want what *they* want and act in ways to get what *they* want. God does not honor that approach because it is ungodly—or, more accurately stated, it is god*less*. It is not the way of God as revealed in Jesus. You're moving in the right direction, Daniel. You've come to the end of yourself—*your* desires, *your* success, *your* accomplishments. You don't care anymore about that, do you?"

"No, ma'am. I honestly only want what God wants. I want to be a means of grace to the world around me."

"Daniel, Ed was right. The foundation is crucial. And the foundation is the Word of God. You're grappling with the nature of God. Go back to our theology classes and conversations. Who is God? Do you remember the Apostles' Creed?"

"He is God, the Father Almighty, Maker of heaven and earth."

"That's right. And that's where we begin. God is the Father, which speaks of his love. God is almighty, which speaks of his power. When love meets power, the result is transformative. God's essence—his divine nature—is holy love. The Old Testament emphasizes God's holiness: 'Be holy because I, the Lord your God, am holy'" (Leviticus 19:2, NIV). "The New Testament emphasizes God's love: 'God is love. Whoever lives in love lives in God, and God in them'" (1 John 4:16, NIV). "Love is the defining essence of the holiness of God. Holiness is the defining essence of the love of God. God is self-giving, holy love. That is crucial to understand, Daniel. And it has implications that must be lived out in the church."

"But what about the justice of God?" Daniel asked. "Many believe God is justice and that his justice governs his love. As I understand that school of thought, the justice of God would limit the love of God."

"That's not what you were taught, Daniel. That's why it doesn't feel right to you. That's why it doesn't make sense to you. If God's justice governs his love, then the character of the community of faith becomes legalistic. If God's essence is justice, then everything is about fair and unfair, rights, and legal claims. But if God's essence is holy love, then holy love limits justice. People don't get what they deserve—they get the expression of holy love that will transform them into the greatest version of their God-created selves. This expression of self-giving holy love is also known as *grace*! Thank God for grace. Grace theology is very different than legalism theology."

Daniel's mental wheels were now spinning in a definite direction. "If God is self-giving, holy love, then the nature of the church should also be characterized by self-giving, holy love. That would mean everything we do must be an expression of the character of God. Everything the church does must be an expression of self-giving, holy love. Our actions must be holy love in action."

"Exactly!" Dr. Darden was excited that her student was internalizing the implications of the God of all grace. "Legalistic systems are expressed through rules and regulations that govern rights and responsibilities. Legalism is transactional. Self-giving, holy love systems are expressed through relationship. Love is transformational."

Daniel was really starting to get it. "In fact, there is no expression of holy love outside the realm of relationships."

"Like I said, you're headed in the right direction. If you want to know what God is like, look at Jesus. Jesus is God in the flesh. He is the Word of God spoken into the world of God. He is holy love in the flesh. We are his body—his hands, feet, mouth, and heartbeat. We, then, are to be God in the world in the flesh. We are to *do* incarnational ministry because we *are* the body of Christ."

Daniel was piecing some of his scattered thoughts together. "That would also mean that justice is about making things right. It is about restoring life the way God intended. And all those efforts must flow from the triune God, who is self-giving, holy love."

"Theology matters, doesn't it! All those hard tests I gave," Dr. Darden continued with a twinkle in her eyes, "were to help you understand that how you interpret Scripture matters. It sets the direction of your specific ministry. Our interpretation of Scripture will determine what types of ministries we initiate and what approaches we take to *doing* church. Theology matters!"

Daniel was thinking out loud now. "We start with the nature of God as we understand it in Scripture. God as self-giving, holy love means we are going to offer grace, love, acceptance, training, accountability, and all that a person needs to be free in Christ. Any ministries we start must grow out of an understanding of the nature of God as self-giving, holy love. That understanding—that theological integrity—should shape our ministries. Then it is not about satisfying the legal God, but it is about living in relationship with the God who loves us."

"Daniel, it goes even deeper than that. That is the way it is expressed, but you also must remember what the Trinity means for us each day."

"Help me think through it, Dr. Darden. What does that look like? What does it mean *practically* speaking? I need a refresher."

"First of all, *God took the initiative in addressing the human predicament.* God created humanity as good. He even called us *good*. The human predicament is brokenness, isolation, and death. Sin entered our world through our disobedience. We forgot who we are and whose we are. That isolated us from God and from each other, left us in a state of brokenness, and resulted in death. So God the Father initiated the redemption plan—the restoration plan. God the Son accomplished it on the cross. And God the Holy Spirit applies it to our lives. Secondly—you know how we theologians like to number our points—*God created us in his image, and his image is communal. We are to live in community with God and with each other.*"

Daniel's pastoral eyes saw a direct application. "Jesus has raised up a new community of people. Race and gender barriers are overcome, then, aren't they? I mean, diversity is not devalued."

Scriptures raced through Daniel's mind, and he began to quote them. 'There is no longer Jew or Greek; there is no longer slave or free; there is no longer male and female, for all of you are one in Christ Jesus'" (Galatians 3:28). "'For he is our peace; in his flesh he has made both into one and has broken down the dividing wall, that is, the hostility between us'" (Ephesians 2:14).

"That's right, Daniel. That's why Jesus summarized the heart of Christianity by saying we shall love the Lord our God with all our heart, soul, mind, and strength and love our neighbors as ourselves" (see Mark 12:30–31). "Let me keep going. *The way the Trinity relates within itself is the model for the way Christians are to relate to one another— and that way is self-giving, holy love.*"

Daniel thought of 1 John 4:7–21:

Beloved, let us love one another, because love is from God; everyone who loves is born of God and knows

God. Whoever does not love does not know God, for God is love. God's love was revealed among us in this way: God sent his only Son into the world so that we might live through him. In this is love, not that we loved God but that he loved us and sent his Son to be the atoning sacrifice for our sins. Beloved, since God loved us so much, we also ought to love one another. No one has ever seen God; if we love one another, God abides in us, and his love is perfected in us.

By this we know that we abide in him and he in us, because he has given us of his Spirit. And we have seen and do testify that the Father has sent his Son as the Savior of the world. God abides in those who confess that Jesus is the Son of God, and they abide in God. So we have known and believe the love that God has for us.

God is love, and those who abide in love abide in God, and God abides in them. Love has been perfected among us in this: that we may have boldness on the day of judgment, because as he is, so are we in this world. There is no fear in love, but perfect love casts out fear; for fear has to do with punishment, and whoever fears has not reached perfection in love. We love because he first loved us. Those who say, "I love God," and hate a brother or sister are liars, for those who do not love a brother or sister, whom they have seen, cannot love God, whom they have not seen. The commandment we have from him is this: those who love God must love their brothers and sisters also.

Again Daniel saw with pastoral eyes. "I treat others as *love* would treat them. I value other people as love would value them. The implication, in a word, is *relationship*—characterized by holy love, the nature of our God."

"Daniel, there is one more incredible implication of the holy love nature of God. *We don't live life alone.* Just as the Trinity is in fellowship, so we are not left alone. In the high priestly prayer Jesus prayed just before his betrayal, arrest, and crucifixion, he prayed for this unity, this relational life for us. Remember?"

Daniel considered John 17:20–26:

> I ask not only on behalf of these but also on behalf of those who believe in me through their word, that they may all be one. As you, Father, are in me and I am in you, may they also be in us, so that the world may believe that you have sent me. The glory that you have given me I have given them, so that they may be one, as we are one, I in them and you in me, that they may become completely one, so that the world may know that you have sent me and have loved them even as you have loved me. Father, I desire that those also, whom you have given me, may be with me where I am, to see my glory, which you have given me because you loved me before the foundation of the world.

> Righteous Father, the world does not know you, but I know you, and these know that you have sent me. I made your name known to them, and I will make it known, so that the love with which you have loved me may be in them and I in them.

"My point is, Daniel, we are *in* Christ, and Christ is *in* the Father, and the Spirit is *in* us, and we are all one—together. We don't live life alone. From the very first chapter of Genesis, when God created humanity in the image of

God (Genesis 1:26–27), to God's promise to Joshua that the Lord would go before and not to be afraid (Deuteronomy 31:8), we are not alone! We live our lives in relationship with God and with one another—a relationship that is characterized by self-giving, holy love."

Daniel had to jump in. "There is empowerment too! When we are *in* Christ and he is *in* us, we are empowered to express his self-giving, holy love *in* the world. Jesus said that all authority had been given to him and by that authority he commanded us to make disciples" (see Matthew 28:18–20). "He is with us, and we live under the banner of his authority. If you pair that with the words of Jesus in Acts 1:8—'But you will receive power when the Holy Spirit has come upon you, and you will be my witnesses in Jerusalem, in all Judea and Samaria, and to the ends of the earth'—it is obvious that the presence of God in our lives brings us the power to be the witnesses of God in this world."

"You got it, Daniel. God is with us both personally and corporately—Father, Son, and Holy Spirit. We do not live life alone."

Daniel began to quote more Scripture that came to mind.

But now, this is what the LORD says—he who created you, Jacob, he who formed you, Israel: "Do not fear, for I have redeemed you; I have summoned you by name; you are mine. When you pass through the waters, I will be with you; and when you pass through the rivers, they will not sweep over you. When you walk through the fire, you will not be burned; the flames will not set you ablaze. For I am the LORD your God, the Holy One of Israel, your Savior."

(Isaiah 43:1–3a, NIV)

As the scripture from Isaiah saturated their hearts, Daniel said pensively, "That means the community of faith—the church—is to be an expression of the presence of God to those who are passing through the waters and the rivers or walking through the fire. God is with us, and we are to be with each other."

"Yes. And don't forget, Daniel, God is with the church and with you as you live into and out of your calling to pastor. You see, if you want to know what the very essence of God means for us, think of it this way: *You and I live our lives engulfed by the holy love of God—God's love for us, our love for one another, and our love for God.* In his essay "Obstinacy in Belief," C. S. Lewis said that we trust not in *a* God but in *this* God."

Daniel said, "The Word is the foundation. And our theological understanding of that Word matters as we move into hands-on ministry. God is with us."

"This is a great cup of coffee, Daniel. I think I'll pour another to take with me."

The rain had stopped, and the sun was peeking through the clouds. Daniel's head was clearing up too. He thought another cup of coffee would do him good as well.

When he walked into the kitchen, he saw a pyramid of cups stacked on the counter. *How did those get there?* "Ah, was Dr. Darden trying to show me a picture, a way of organizing these thoughts?" An image began to form in Daniel's mind that would need some exploration as his trip unfolded.

5

WHO ARE YOU, AND WHAT ARE YOU DOING HERE?

With lunch over and his hunger satisfied, Daniel decided to hike to a section of the valley that looked intriguing. The cooler, rainy morning had given way to a gloriously sunny afternoon. The thought occurred to him that the creek running by the house just might flow into a little swimming hole. His love for creeks got the best of him, so he put on his shorts and set out on another adventure.

Daniel followed the creek, walking beside it for a considerable distance. He looked back and could no longer see the house. Looking ahead, he saw a bend. The creek had been growing steadily wider, and as it turned left, it created a perfect swimming hole, complete with a high bank, a shade tree, and a rope swing. Who could ask for anything more on such a beautiful day!

Peeling off his shirt and laying it beside his shoes on the bank, Daniel waded into the deeper water, checking for stumps or other dangerous underwater obstacles that might do him harm. Since there was a rope swing, he surmised there would be nothing in the landing area, and his suspicions were confirmed. He couldn't wait to swing and drop.

He climbed out on the bank, gripped the rope in his hands, pushed off, and swung out over the water. His "yee-haw" could be heard all over the valley as he hit the cold water of the mountain stream. There were few things more refreshing than swimming in a mountain stream. But it was cold!

Daniel thought of his family back home. *My kids would love this! I'm coming back to this place with them.* He could envision Erin, Caroline, and Charlie swinging on the rope and playing in the creek. He could taste the picnic Erin would prepare and imagine the fun they would have. *Definitely! I'll be back.*

Lying on the sunny bank in soft grass and staring up at the blue sky, Daniel was drying out and dreaming of his family when his mind turned to the reason he was here in the first place. "Well, if for no other purpose, this is one good thing coming from my trip." Even as he spoke, he knew the trip had already been worth it. What he'd learned from his conversations with Sam, Ed, and Dr. Darden was worth the price of admission. Yet he knew there was more.

Daniel's thoughts about his experiences thus far were interrupted by the clearing of a throat. Startled, he turned to see none other than Sam standing there. "Hi, Sam. I didn't expect to see you again, but I'm sure glad I did!" Daniel knew it was useless to try to guess where Sam had been or where he came from. He just accepted the fact that he was there with him in that moment. Daniel geared himself up to learn more from his new friend.

"Are you enjoying your stay at the cabin, Daniel? You came at the perfect time. Of course, there is no bad time up here. Being out in God's creation is always good. Kind of like God himself—the atmosphere is saturated with a sense of holy love, wouldn't you say?"

"Sam, I've been doing a lot of thinking on this trip. I've asked God to search my heart and mind and give me wisdom to know what I should do. I feel like I'm moving in the right direction, but I also know there are so many more changes I need to make. I'm worrying over this like a dog with a bone, and I know God is going to help me figure it out. Any suggestions?"

"Sure. I'm not the answer man, but I may be the question man. I think we need to start by asking the right questions. Do you remember what I asked you when we met? I told you I knew your story, but I asked you 'who are you, and what are you doing here?' Let's start with that. I think that might put us on the right track. Who are you, Daniel? Who has God called you to be?"

Daniel replied, "I don't think you're asking what I *do*. You reminded me that we are to *be* before we are to *do*. The answer I *want* to give is that I am a pastor."

"That's right. But, before you are a pastor, you are a person created in the image of God, a person belonging to God, a person whom God has chosen to *be* a pastor. It is *who* God has called, graced, equipped, and empowered you to *be*. So let's take a look at that role. Let's work backwards—or, rather, start on the surface and dig down through the layers. What do you do as a pastor, Daniel?"

"I preach. I teach. I lead meetings. I visit people in hospitals, conduct funerals and weddings, counsel people going through difficulties. The list is pretty long and diverse. Is that what you're asking?"

47

"Yes. Let's keep digging. Think of it this way: you are charged with being a leader in the church. Jesus is the head of the church, so he becomes the prototype for you. Remember, it's all about God. Who is Jesus? Besides the fact that he is the Son of God—God incarnate—he also fulfills the roles of *prophet, priest,* and *king.* I'm sure Dr. Darden taught you this in Christology. Let's take those roles as the archetype for your role as pastor."

"How do you define a prophet?" Daniel asked.

Sam must have spent time in a classroom because he launched into lecture mode. "A prophet is called by God to proclaim the Word of God to the people of God for the sake of the world of God. Historically, many of them looked strange and acted in ways that caused people to raise an eyebrow. Their behavior was often symbolic of what God was trying to communicate to the people. But the core function of the prophet was to proclaim the Word of the Lord.

"And not everyone liked the prophets," Sam added. "In fact, most prophets were killed at worst, or disregarded at best—until their Word from the Lord came to pass. A prophet stood apart from the authority of the community to a certain degree and communicated the passion of God in judgment against evil. The people didn't really want to hear from the prophets. There were people in authority who tried to silence the prophets or at least control what they said. But the prophets were answerable to God, not to the people. The prophets called the people to repentance and offered the invitation to renew their covenantal relationship with God."

Daniel, remembering his Old Testament theology, chimed in, "The prophets seemed to feel the passion of God and the expression of his holy love toward the disobedient and disenfranchised. The prophets continuously challenged the people to be the faithful people of God, faithful to the covenant God had made with them."

"The prophet," Sam said, "proclaimed the God of the kingdom—sometimes in confrontational ways."

"Jesus did that," Daniel said. "He proclaimed the kingdom of God, the will of God, and the ways of God. And sometimes that involved confronting sin and those who found themselves in opposition to God and his nature of self-giving, holy love."

"Remember, too, Daniel, the authorities crucified him. But God raised him up and validated his Word."

Daniel said, "Okay. Now what about a *priest*?"

Sam paused to let Daniel think about the answer to his own question. "What did priests do, Daniel?"

"Well, they seemed to be different than the prophets. Their function was to mediate between God and his people. They represented the people to God and God to the people in a different way than the prophets. They were more community-oriented."

Sam added, "That's right. In fact, a priest would find definition and function *only in community*. If you don't have a people, you're not a priest. You could be an outcast and be a prophet, but you had to have a flock to be a shepherd. Priests lead people in connecting with God. They direct people in worship."

Daniel again thought about Jesus. "Jesus did that too. He even called himself the Good Shepherd. He connected people with God. The letter to the Hebrews calls him the great high priest because of how he fulfilled this role" (see Hebrews 4:14). "In fact, the Word tells us he is at the right hand of the Father interceding for us right now."

"Daniel, I know you're on a soul-searching quest. But remember this: Jesus is praying for you even as we speak."

Tears filled Daniel's eyes as he thought of all the painful and difficult situations he faced. The questions and doubts that had driven him to these hills moved to the forefront of his mind as he allowed the depth of his agony to surface. Those issues were confronted with the truth that Jesus was praying for him even now. "God cares. And why wouldn't he? It is *who* he is—holy love! He is the Good Father, and we are loved by him. Jesus is the Great High Priest!"

After a moment of reflection Daniel turned to Sam and said, "What about *king*? Pastors certainly aren't kings. In fact, that's half our problem—we act as if we're building our own kingdoms, or at least our own little fiefdoms within God's kingdom. I'm not a king, nor do I want to be."

Sam said, "Think about the true role of a king. A king is a leader. A king administrates the kingdom. A king deals with issues like vision and direction."

Daniel, still not comfortable with the word, said, "Kingships are often wrapped up in power. Where does power come into the mix?"

"Kings do hold power. But they also *give* power. Think about the role of king as one who empowers people to act. A king oversees the training of the army, the education and equipping of the people within the kingdom."

"I'm starting to see it. It's not about me *being* king but about the functions the king fulfills, particularly related to equipping and empowering people to use their talents and abilities."

"Yes. A king sets the context for the people to be and do what they were created to be and do. And," Sam continued, "don't leave out organizational issues along with leadership and administration. Those roles must be fulfilled as well." Knowing how Daniel's mind was turning, Sam asked, "Did Jesus do that as well?"

"Absolutely! He was *the* King! He had the power and authority, and he gave it to his disciples. They in turn ministered under the banner of the authority of the King. The Great Commission comes to mind. And in Acts 1:8 Jesus told his followers to wait for power. He knew they needed to be empowered for the purpose of missional effectiveness."

"What about leadership?" Sam asked.

"Jesus was the consummate leader. He invited people to follow him. He even said, 'I will *make you* fishers of people. We follow, but *he* educates, equips, and empowers us."

"Sounds like a three-point sermon, Daniel. Did Jesus administrate?"

"Hmm? Well, I think so. Yes. There seemed to be organization to his band of followers. Peter, James, and John appeared to be his right-hand people. He also had a treasurer, and he made sure his taxes were paid. All administrative."

"Now, let's take the tasks you do and group them according to the archetype given to us by the functions of Jesus."

Daniel thought for a few moments and then started in. "Under the function of *prophet,* I preach and teach the Word of God. I address issues that deal with how the church lives as the people of God. I call people to be faithful to our relationship with God, living like Christ in the world around us. Sometimes what I address in preaching is confrontational. Sometimes I have to address the ways we are not like Christ in our individual lives and as a church body. Not fun, but necessary."

"The reason it's necessary is that it flows from who you are—pastor," Sam added.

Daniel continued, "I fulfill the function of priest when I visit the sick or counsel people walking through challenges. Sometimes it is helpful to folks when I simply listen to their issues and then carry those before God in prayer. I think I fulfill this role when I lead worship too, administering the sacraments and praying over our people."

"That's all part of it," Sam said. "Don't forget about weddings, funerals, and informal conversations that encourage folks."

Daniel remembered a recent episode in the church. "A few weeks ago there was an issue causing conflict in the church body. People were starting to choose sides and polarize. I recognized the situation and pulled the groups together to look at all sides. We left the meeting with greater understanding and a sense of unity. Is that one of the priestly functions?"

"You're right on target. The priest cares for the needs of the community of faith. You are to help establish community, intimacy, relationship, and common feeling. And the priest has to deal with conflict as it arises. As the shepherd of the flock, you have to protect the flock. Conflict can result in harm to the flock if it is not properly handled."

Daniel moved to his next category. "On my *king* list are items like leading the ministerial staff and lay leaders, which involves delegating, training, and equipping."

Sam said, "There's a difference between empowering people to serve and assigning them a job. The former is true delegation while the latter is dumping. Simply giving people a job to do, with no consideration of their giftedness, abilities, passion, or experiences is to set them up for failure. God doesn't treat us that way, and we should not treat others that way. Empowerment at its most basic level involves giving people power. That means training, educating, equipping, and authorizing them to do the ministry—a big task."

Daniel chimed in, "Equipping—now that's a *huge* task!"

Sam reached into the depths of his knowledge of Scripture and said, "Did you realize that the only time the word 'pastor' appears in the New Testament, it is tied to equipping? Ephesians 4:11–12 says, 'So Christ himself gave the apostles, the prophets, the evangelists, the pastors and teachers, to equip his people for works of service, so that the body of Christ may be built up.'"

Daniel kept thinking out loud. "That reminds me of the benediction in the letter to the Hebrews: 'Now may the God of peace, who brought back from the dead our Lord Jesus, the great shepherd of the sheep, by the blood of the eternal covenant, make you complete in everything good so that you may do his will, as he works among us that which is pleasing in his sight, through Jesus Christ, to whom be the glory forever. Amen'" (13:20–21).

"You're on the right track, Daniel. Don't forget what kind of king Jesus is. He is a servant-king. Not the kind who lords it over others. He uses his authority to serve. You know, he is even called the Suffering Servant. That's connected to his kingly authority."

"On my list in all caps is the word EQUIPPER," Daniel said.

"Daniel, you remember our discussion of doing something *for* God versus letting God work *through* you? Just as God has gifted and graced you, he has done the same for all people. Pastors who do everything themselves rob others of the privilege of using their gifts and graces for God. That's one reason many followers are either spiritually immature or extremely frustrated."

"What do you mean?"

"Think about it. If you have a child and you do everything for that child from spoon-feeding him and tying his shoes to cleaning his room, that child will never learn and grow. It's one thing if the child is an infant. But it's quite another when the child is fifteen. As a matter of fact, if you had a fifteen-year-old son who couldn't feed himself, tie his shoes, or clean his room, you'd think something was delayed developmentally."

"I see what you mean. If I, as pastor, do everything for my people and don't allow them—"

"—*Equip* them," Sam interrupted.

"—If I don't *equip* them," Daniel corrected, "in the use of their gifts in service with God, then I'm hindering their spiritual development and their walk with God."

"Exactly! What you need to remember is that people are *gifted* by the Holy Spirit, *valuable* to the advancement of the kingdom of Christ, and *empowered* to serve God as God intends. These are the theological affirmations for lay leadership. Add to these the belief that every believer is a minister and every ministry is important. All these factors work in harmony as we remember we are *dependent on one another in order for us all to reach our potential.*"

Daniel turned again to the foundation of the Word he and Ed had discussed a couple days ago. "That sounds like what Paul intended in Ephesians 4:11–16:

He himself granted that some are apostles, prophets, evangelists, pastors and teachers to equip the saints for the work of ministry, for building up the body of

Christ, until all of us come to the unity of the faith and of the knowledge of the Son of God, to maturity, to the measure of the full stature of Christ. We must no longer be children, tossed to and fro and blown about by every wind of doctrine by people's trickery, by their craftiness in deceitful scheming; but speaking the truth in love, we must grow up in every way into him who is the head, into Christ, from whom the whole body, joined and knit together by every ligament with which it is equipped, as each part is working properly, promotes the body's growth in building itself up in love.

"Exactly," affirmed Sam. "I can tell you're a little uncomfortable using the word 'king' to identify part of the role of pastor. It's easy to revert to the parody of a king instead of understanding God's intentions. Use the word 'equipper' if you like that better. It's what you do: equip, empower, encourage, and release people to serve out of their own gifts and graces.

"There is another very important piece to this, Daniel. In your strategies for ministry, you must get the right people in place. The right people will create the most effective strategies for ministry. Most people think you get the plan first, but generally you need the right people in place who will then create the right culture. The right strategies will flow from the right people and the right culture. This is an art more than a science."

These concepts clarified for Daniel much of the confusion he had experienced in his job as a pastor. It had become just that—a job. That's not what he had expected or wanted, nor what he felt deep down in his soul that pastoring was intended to be. Yet he had not been able to get his mind around all the complexities of being a pastor.

Daniel zoned out for a moment, staring at the serene landscape and sensing the peace that passes understanding as it drifted through his mind like the gentle breeze from the creek. *Pastor as prophet, priest, and equipper. I can get my mind around this,* he thought. There was a feeling of rightness in thinking of who he was and what he was to do that flowed from this paradigm.

An idea popped into his head. Perhaps when he returned to the cabin he would make a list of all he did as pastor and categorize each one under the heading of Prophet, Priest, or Equipper. It would be interesting to see it all spelled out on paper—and even to see what he did that he shouldn't be doing because it was beyond the core of who he was and what he was meant to do.

6

WHO ARE Y'ALL, AND WHAT ARE Y'ALL DOING HERE?

"We're not through for the day, Daniel."

The statement startled Daniel back to reality—at least, this valley's version of reality. How long had he been lost in contemplation about his own role as prophet, priest, and equipper? He wasn't sure, and it didn't matter.

Sam continued. "The same question we just explored about who you are must also be asked in relation to the church. Who is the church—the plural you? Since we're in the Smoky Mountains—who are *y'all*, and what are *y'all* doing here?"

"Come on, Sam, everyone knows who . . . what . . . who . . . the church is."

"Really? I can hear your struggle in referring to it as *who* or *what*," Sam said with a grin. "It's not as common of an understanding as you might think. You must know who the church is if you're going to be a leader in . . . it."

Sam started preaching again. "That's part of the problem today. The church is experiencing an identity crisis.

Ministers, pastors, church leaders—people who are supposed to know—aren't really sure who the church is, so they struggle to lead the church. Pastors and churches today try any and everything. The church's identity crisis has resulted in many departures from theological affirmations. People have tried to reshape God into their image rather than live into the image of God. Many churches are driven by subconscious forces focused on personal success. They walk away from practices that should be retained and cling to practices that should be discarded. Pastors are notorious for copying the latest success story from across the country in cultural contexts very different from their own. Why? Because they do not know who they are as pastors or who the people of God are from God's perspective."

"I didn't realize the implications of our identity crisis," Daniel bemoaned. "I guess it has far-reaching ramifications, creating a cacophony of challenges today. Who are we as the church, Sam?"

"Why ask me?" Sam responded with a mischievous grin on his face. "Remember the foundation? Go to the Word, Daniel. What does the Word have to say about who the church is? Need a Bible?"

Daniel obviously hadn't brought his Bible when he set out to explore the creek, so Sam produced a Bible and handed it to him. Daniel began to search passages he thought might be helpful. He used the concordance in the back of the Bible to help guide him along. He wished he had his computer with him now. His software with the Greek and Hebrew search engines would be extremely helpful. But he had to go with the basics. Maybe the basics would be enough for now.

"Here's a word that describes the church, Sam. 'Fellowship.' In Greek it is *koinonia* and means a partnership, a social interaction for a specific purpose. It carries the idea of communion, or community. It involves participation in the life of the church. Let me read some places it's found. Acts 2:42: 'They devoted themselves to the apostles' teaching and *fellowship*, to the breaking of bread and the prayers.' Philippians 1:3–6: 'I thank my God for every remembrance of you, always in every one of my prayers for all of you, praying with joy for your *partnership* in the gospel from the first day until now. I am confident of this, that the one who began a good work in you will continue to complete it until the day of Jesus Christ.' And 1 John 1:3: 'What we have seen and heard we also declare to you so that you also may have *fellowship* with us, and truly our *fellowship* is with the Father and with his Son Jesus Christ.'"

Daniel thought of another word. "What about the actual word 'church'? In Greek it is *ecclesia*. It was used by Jesus when Peter confessed him to be the Messiah. Matthew 16:18: 'And I tell you, you are Peter, and on this rock I will build my *church*, and the gates of Hades will not prevail against it.' *Ecclesia* refers to a called-out group of people."

"That's right, Daniel, but remember they are called out *for a particular purpose*. It is translated in 1 Peter as 'God's own people.'"

"Here it is." Daniel read the scripture from 1 Peter 2:9: 'But you are a chosen people, a royal priesthood, a holy nation, *God's own people*, in order that you may proclaim the excellence of him who called you out of darkness into his marvelous light.'"

Daniel kept thinking. "There is also 'the body of Christ.' Let's see where that phrase is found. How about Romans

12:4–6: 'For as in one *body* we have many members and not all the members have the same function, so we, who are many, are one *body* in Christ, and individually we are members one of another. We have gifts that differ according to the grace given to us: prophecy, in proportion to faith.' Or there's 1 Corinthians 12:27: 'Now you are the *body* of Christ and individually members of it.' Or listen to Ephesians 4:11– 13: 'He himself granted that some are apostles, prophets, evangelists, pastors and teachers to equip the saints for the work of ministry, for building up the *body* of Christ, until all of us come to the unity of the faith and of the knowledge of the Son of God, to maturity, to the measure of the full stature of Christ.'"

Daniel continued, "I also remember from my theology classes that you can't really speak of the church apart from the concept of covenant, which is person-centered. Relationship provides the context for the covenant. Jesus entered into covenant with us. He said as much in Luke 22:20 at the Passover meal he shared with his disciples: 'This cup is the new covenant in my blood, which is poured out for you'" (NIV).

"That's right, Daniel. Now, follow up your scriptural foundation with your theological interpretation. What does theology have to say about who the church is?" Sam was helping Daniel see how to think pastorally and intentionally when trying to develop answers to perplexing questions.

"Let's see. I think I can recall what is classically referred to as 'the marks of the church': unity, universality (also called catholicity), holiness (characterized by self-giving love), apostolicity (bearing witness to the resurrection of Christ), and word and sacrament."

Sam added to the theological conversation, impressing Daniel with his knowledge of various theologians. "Martin Luther defined the church in terms of its gospel. He said, 'The church is where the Word is rightly preached and the sacraments rightly administered.' And John Wesley described the church as 'a company of [those] called by the gospel, grafted into Christ by baptism, animated by love, united by all kind of fellowship, and disciplined by the death of Ananias and Sapphira.' The Ananias and Sapphira phrase used to confuse me until I understood it in the context of accountability. The church has the element of accountable relationships. Accountability is an integral aspect of the church."

Daniel's mind was slightly overloaded, trying to wrap itself around all these concepts of church. "How can I summarize that, Sam? Do you have a good definition of the church? Can you succinctly tell me who we are?"

"Not totally succinct, but try this out for size: *The church is a covenantal community of people called out of their former life of sin and brokenness and into the life of Jesus for the purpose of advancing the kingdom of God (characterized by self-giving, holy love). We are the body of Christ doing the transformational work of Christ in the world around us.*"

There is a world of meaning behind each phrase, Daniel thought.

As if Sam could read his mind, he said, "You can just say 'church' or 'body of Christ' if you'd like, but now you know who we are."

"Sam, there is still more to this, isn't there? I mean, we said earlier the terms and phrases identifying the church implied being called out for a specific purpose. There was a reason for the fellowship. Jesus entered into the new covenant with a definite mission in view."

"Keep unpacking it, Daniel. Once you understand who you are and who the church is, you will naturally ask another very important question—"

"What is the mission of the church?" Daniel interrupted as if he couldn't wait to give a good answer.

"Well, not exactly," Sam replied.

Daniel was disappointed. He thought he knew where Sam was going.

"You're going down the right path, but pastors often believe the myth that the church has a mission. The truth is that God is the One with the mission, and he calls the church to participate in it. Someone once said, 'The church doesn't have a mission; the mission has a church.' The church was made for God's mission, the *missio Dei*, not the other way around. Remember, it is all about God and his will, his plans, his reconciling the world to himself through Christ. One of the problems in Christianity today is that there are too many independent missions that are isolated from the mission of God."

"Mission," Daniel said reflectively, almost under his breath. "That is a buzzword today, a hot topic of conversation—but I just thought mission statements were like slogans. I didn't put much emphasis on them."

"That's where I would challenge your thinking, Daniel. Mission is huge! Once you understand the foundation of the Word of God and the necessity of theological integrity, the next most important issue to delve into is *mission*. Jesus has invited us—the church, the body of Christ—to join *his* mission in the world. In fact, what the church *does* must flow from who the church *is*. And the church's identity—who it is—is based on the Trinity. You see, Daniel, it all starts with Jesus—with Christology. Then it moves to Jesus's mission in the world—missiology. Then it moves to Jesus's followers known as the church—ecclesiology. It's Jesus, then his mission, then his church."

"Sam, it seems to me like the church has this out of order. Every church today has a mission. Each church tries to say it differently than other churches. It's as if uniqueness gets points for the afterlife. Looking at all the various mission statements, I could conclude that either God is rather scattered in his thinking, or mission is just a human idea of what each church or pastor *wants* to do."

"Not really. You're making a mistake that many leaders make. Don't confuse *mission* with mission *statement*. A statement is simply a synopsis or summary of what you are about—a way of stating your *obsession*. People can articulate the same concepts in a variety of ways. They can use words or images that resonate with them and their specific culture. However, there is a consistent mission in the mind of God, and his church must join him in his mission. I think of a mission statement or image—some churches are not using words now, but images—as symbols revealing meaning far deeper than just the statement. I look at a mission as a boundary that keeps me focused on the things that matter most," Sam explained further. "God has a mission. He has a task, a job to do, a charge to keep. Whatever you want to call it, God has set his divine mind to this mission. He is all in on his mission. He used words—that's why we have the Word of the Lord. He used images—think of the cross or the empty tomb. Everything God does is based on his mission, which, by the way, flows out of *who he is*—self-giving, holy love."

"What is God's mission in the world? How would you articulate that, Sam?"

"The mission of God, theologically referred to as *missio Dei*, is revealed in the Word of God. In the garden of Eden, after the fall of humanity, God came looking for Adam and Eve. They were feeling isolated, fearful, and guilty. They knew shame for the first time. They had lived life, and now they were living death. All types of analogies have been used. The point is that God came to them. Religion is about human beings trying to get to God. Christianity is about God coming to us. The mission of God is about God entering the world. God is still entering the lives of the isolated, the fearful, the guilty, the shamed, and the dying."

"As you say that, Sam, I think of major events or statements in Scripture. In Genesis 12, God calls Abram to follow him. Where? Into the world. And God promises to bless all the peoples of the earth through an obedient, faithful Abram. God's mission was to transform the world through a chosen person."

Sam added, "You can even think of God putting the world back in order. Or you might say that God's mission is to restore the world to its original condition, just as he intended in creation."

Daniel continued with of the concept of mission. "Then, moving forward in time, God wanted to accomplish the same mission through the people of Israel. It was God's mission to restore the world to his original intent and do that through his chosen people. They did not fulfill that role, but still their failure did not deter God from his mission. Jesus told Nicodemus in John 3:16–17: 'For God so loved the world that he gave his only Son, so that everyone who believes in him may not perish but may have eternal life. Indeed, God did not send the Son into the world to condemn the world but in order that the world might be saved through him.' Even though I learned that verse as a child in Sunday school, its theological and missional significance is certainly not childish."

Sam helped Daniel recall the words of Jesus. "Think of what Jesus said when the Pharisees criticized him for eating with sinners: 'Those who are well have no need of a physician, but those who are sick. Go and learn what this means, "I desire mercy, not sacrifice." For I have not come to call the righteous but sinners'" (Matthew 9:12–13).

Now Daniel was even more into this concept. "Jesus said he came to seek and save what was lost" (Luke 19:10). "And in Luke 15, he told parables of the searching God."

"Don't forget about Paul. He understood the mission of God in the world. He used terms like 'redemption,' 'justification,' and 'sanctification.' He said in Colossians 1:13–14, 'He has rescued us from the power of darkness and transferred us into the kingdom of his beloved Son, in whom we have redemption, the forgiveness of sins.'"

In essence, Daniel was getting his mind around things. "God is about restoration. God's mission is to restore us to life. His mission flows from who he is. Holy love can't leave us in our broken, lost, isolated bondage. God took the initiative to . . . *save* us. 'Save' is a good word."

"'Save' *is* a good word," Sam echoed with a tear in his eye. "God saves us through entering into our world, in the flesh, in the form of a human being, to transform us, restore us, give us life—the expressions of holy love go on and on."

Daniel was overwhelmed by the love of God as his mind was bombarded by the Word of God—the same Word he had preached for years:

I came that they may have life and have it abundantly. (John 10:10b)

For while we were still weak, at the right time Christ died for the ungodly. Indeed, rarely will anyone die for a righteous person—though perhaps for a good person someone might actually dare to die. But God proves his love for us in that while we still were sinners Christ died for us.
(Romans 5:6–8)

But when the fullness of time had come, God sent his Son, born of a woman, born under the law, in order to redeem those who were under the law, so that we might receive adoption as children. (Galatians 4:4–5)

God made him who had no sin to be sin for us, so that in him we might become the righteousness of God.
(2 Corinthians 5:21, NIV)

Consequently, he is able for all time to save those who approach God through him, since he always lives to make intercession for them.
(Hebrews 7:25)

But this is the covenant that I will make with the house of Israel after those days, says the LORD: I will put my law within them, and I will write it on their hearts, and I will be their God, and they shall be my people. No longer shall they teach one another or say to each other, "Know the LORD," for they shall all know me, from the least of them to the greatest, says the LORD, for I will forgive their iniquity and remember their sin no more.
(Jeremiah 31:33–34)

Sam let the moment of grace sink into Daniel's soul. This was part of the refreshing Daniel desperately needed. "God has come to make the world *right* again. His mission is to restore order out of our chaos. Only a God who is self-giving, holy love would choose to love the unlovable."

Now tears were in Daniel's eyes, and he spoke reflectively. "God has a mission. He moves into the world to save the world from itself. He moves into our lives to save us from ourselves. God took the initiative. The Word became flesh. God came to us in the form of the Son. He knew the forces of evil had to be defeated and that the battleground was the cross. So he took on the full force of evil—everything that evil could throw at him. He allowed himself to be crucified because of his self-giving, holy love for all creation, fighting and dying on our behalf. God raised Jesus from the dead to reveal his victory over evil. Now the Holy Spirit applies the victory to our lives—to my life, to my family's lives, to the lives of the people I serve as pastor, to the lives of people I don't even know, to the lives of people very different from me. Life can be *right* because God is self-giving, holy Love."

"It really is all about God and his mission in the world," Sam summarized.

"You said the church does not really have a mission of its own but is to engage in the mission of God."

"That's right, Daniel. God accomplishes his mission through the church. It really is through Jesus, but remember that the church is the body of Christ in the world today. As God sent his Son into the world, Jesus sends his church into the world. The church is sent because God is a sending God."

"Well, that is consistent with 1 John 4:17, 'as he is, so are we in this world.'"

Sam continued, "Did you realize that the word 'mission' comes from the Latin *mittere*, which means 'to send'? God is a sending God. He sent his Son. And now he sends his church, empowered by the Holy Spirit. Remember what Jesus said to his disciples after the resurrection? 'As the Father has sent me, so I send you'" (John 20:21b). "And don't forget what Paul wrote to the believers in Corinth: 'All this is from God, who reconciled us to himself through Christ and has given us the ministry of reconciliation; that is, in Christ God was reconciling the world to himself, not counting their trespasses against them, and entrusting the message of reconciliation to us. So we are ambassadors for Christ, since God is making his appeal through us; we entreat you on behalf of Christ: be reconciled to God. For our sake God made the one who knew no sin to be sin, so that in him we might become the righteousness of God'" (2 Corinthians 5:18–21).

"My theological teaching is coming back to me," Daniel said. "I remember learning that the church is to be witnesses of the kingdom of God. This is done by living like the King and participating in his mission in the world. Some of my profs said the church is to advance the kingdom of God in the world. I heard N. T. Wright say once that the church is to so live in this world that the people of this world and the forces of evil know there is another king, and his name is Jesus."

"Your professors were right on target with the Word of the Lord and good theological interpretation. Some Christian leaders get it backwards. They think a mission comes from the church. In reality, the church exists because God has a mission."

"Sam, are there any specific tracks for the mission train to run on? Any practical ways of thinking about this ministry?"

"Sure. Go back to the Word. God communicated his expectations in Deuteronomy and Leviticus. His Word was summarized by Israelite theologians and quoted by Jesus. Love the Lord your God with all your heart and with all your soul and with all your mind and love your neighbor as yourself. Jesus said, 'All the Law and the Prophets hang on these two commandments'" (Matthew 22:40, NIV). "He was, of course, referring to Deuteronomy 6:5 and Leviticus 19:18. And don't forget," Sam continued, "how God called Abram to leave and follow so God could bless the world. That was the Old Testament parallel to the Great Commission. Embedded in these scriptures are the tracks of worship, discipleship, evangelism, compassionate ministry, global missions, and community life with believers."

"I see compassionate ministry in the parable of the Good Samaritan too," Daniel interjected. "And in the parable in Matthew about the sheep and the goats, where Jesus said, 'Just as you did it to one of the least of these brothers and sisters of mine, you did it to me'" (Matthew 25:40). "And Paul talked about community life in Galatians 6:10: 'So then, whenever we have an opportunity, let us work for the good of all and especially for those of the family of faith.' He also said in Galatians 6:2 that we should carry each other's burdens and in so doing we fulfill the will of Christ. Oh, and what Jesus said in John 13:34–35 is crucial! 'I give you a new commandment, that you love one another. Just as I have loved you, you also should love one another. By this everyone will know that you are my disciples, if you have love for one another.'"

"Daniel, those are the tracks the mission train can run on. Those tracks allow the mission of God to be expressed specifically in the world. They keep the church from losing its focus. They help the people of God keep the main thing the main thing. If church leaders are not intentionally focused on the mission of God, they tend to focus on goals that are not at the heart of God's mission. It can easily degenerate into personal goals, ambitions, and dreams."

Daniel said, "God's mission is to restore the world—to make it *right* again. In fact, you could say that God's mission is to redeem, restore, recreate, and renew the whole of creation, making it all *right* once more. And he is sending the church into the world to join him as he works missionally through the Holy Spirit. The way the church can begin to get a handle on this is to think specifically in terms of worship, compassionate ministry, community life, discipleship, evangelism, and global missions. Am I on the right path?" Daniel wanted to get it straight in his mind.

"You're getting there," Sam reassured him. "You can think of the *missio Dei* as the what *generally* speaking, and you can think of the purposes, or tracks, as the what *specifically* speaking."

Daniel sat deep in thought near the creek for a few moments. Finally he spoke. "It's still a little vague. Remember, as a pastor, I'm a practitioner first. How do we get this into a system that accomplishes the mission of God?"

Sam didn't answer.

Daniel looked around. Gone again. "That man shows up and disappears before I even know it," Daniel mused. "Oh well. God will help me figure this out. Right now the rope swing needs me on it, and the creek needs me in it. Yee-haw!"

Later, Daniel returned to the cabin after he finished swimming and playing in the creek. He felt so relaxed! In fact, he couldn't even remember the last time he had been this relaxed. He stepped up on the porch and suddenly realized just how tired he really was. *A late afternoon nap is just what the doctor ordered*, Daniel thought. He headed straight to the screened section of the porch, plopped down on the swing, and was soon peacefully asleep.

Just how long Daniel slept he wasn't sure. But the sun was setting as he stood up and stretched. He should be hungry, but he was hungrier to process the idea of a mission statement for his church. Grabbing his computer, he went to the little table on the back patio and started typing.

Now that Daniel understood who created the church, who the church is, what the church is to do, and the target of its ministries, it was simply a matter of articulating a statement to that fact. The mission statement needed to contain, or at least unpack, the purposes of the church in some form. He began to formulate ideas and concepts, researching acronyms and images. He searched the web, saw what other churches had written, and searched Scripture for key words.

In the end he decided this task was not meant to be done on the back porch of a cabin in the mountains but rather was to be accomplished in community. Daniel decided that, when he returned, he would gather a group of creative leaders in the church who would be passionate about formulating a mission statement together. He would bring them up to speed on the theological musings he and Sam had worked through together. Then they would write a mission statement that communicated a biblical understanding of the *missio Dei* and the purposes God intended for their local church in their cultural context. And, he thought, it would be good to include the core values in the document.

Suddenly Daniel realized he was indeed hungry. Supper after a full day, time on the back porch listening to the sounds of the night, and a good night's sleep would equip him for whatever adventure came his way tomorrow. Wow! What a trip!

7

GETTING IT ALL STRAIGHTENED OUT

What a great night of sleep! Knowing who you are and why you're here brings a sense of peace deep down in the soul.

As Daniel lay in bed thinking about the events of the week, he began to hear noises from the other end of the house. *What in the world could that be?* he wondered.

Daniel climbed out of bed and walked into the family room to find his notes scattered all over the floor. *How? What?* Then he noticed that he'd left the back door ajar. Cabinets stood open, food was all over the place, and the house was generally a mess. *It will take me hours to get this place straightened up!*

Suddenly, his eyes located the culprit, a raccoon. Daniel remembered reading somewhere that raccoons could be rather dangerous. As cute as they are, their face mask is indicative of their nature—little bandits that will hurt you if you get in their way.

Daniel knew he had to get the little varmint out of the house, but how? Should he whistle, try to startle it, shout at it? Finally he decided to leave the back door open, slip into the kitchen where the raccoon was still enjoying breakfast, and herd him out. Somehow it worked, and now he had to go to work straightening up the mess the creature had made.

When the job was complete and Daniel had his cup of coffee and was heading to the back porch to start on his notes, the truth of the experience dawned on him like the arrival of a new day: organization! "What I need to do is get organized!" Three words immediately came to mind: *missional, teleological,* and *practical.*

Daniel began to play with the words. The first was now straightforward. After his last conversation with Sam, he knew what it meant to be missional. The organizational system had to be built on the mission—obviously not just any mission but the mission of God in the world and his intended purposes through the church for the world. He recalled the proper order: God has a mission in the world to accomplish through the church. In order to be *missional,* the organizational system itself needed to be constructed around the major missional components.

Teleological was a concept from his studies in Greek and theology. The Greek word for completion, for fulfilling one's intended purpose, was *teleos.* For something to be teleological meant it led to a desired end, a goal intended from the beginning. Teleological implies that there is an identified goal and a plan to move toward it. The organizational system needed to be teleological—designed in such a way that, if implemented, it would cause the organization to move toward the desired goal.

"What is that desired goal? Is it not the mission of God to restore the world?" Daniel realized that various pieces of this week were falling into place. He spoke aloud to himself. "Being teleological is tied to being missional. In other words, the organizational system needs to move the organization— wait a minute—it needs to allow people to *become* what God intended (Christlike) and *do* what God intended (join him in his work to restore all creation). Okay. *Teleological.*"

Practical. *Now that's a word I get. I am a practitioner,* Daniel thought. It needs to work. It needs to be workable, manageable, easy to follow, and doable in the context of a local church. People are busy with life. They have families, jobs, hobbies—the list is endless. People are involved in the life of their local culture, as they should be. Their local culture is where people build relationships with the people God seeks to redeem. The organizational structure needs to be something people can follow in everyday life.

Ideas and images began to form in his mind. Most organizations think from the top down. Daniel had seen his share of organizational structures from his reading in leadership. He began to draw a model of what he had seen in the past—the most common organizational structure.

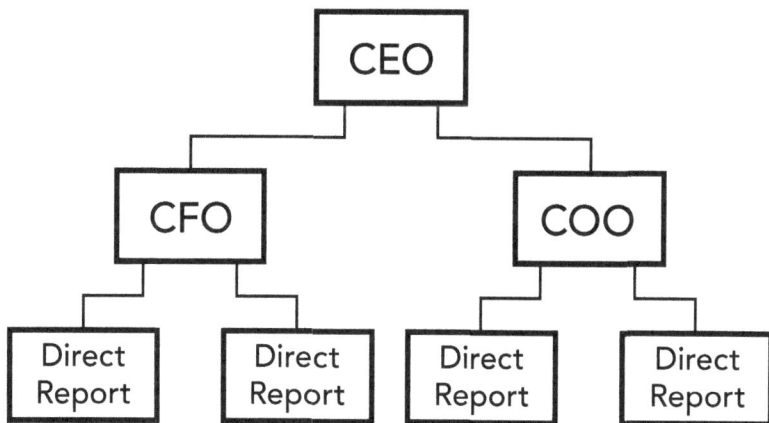

"This traditional model is inadequate. It doesn't really convey the crucial missional or teleological character. What about . . . ?" Daniel again began to draw, but this time the result looked very different. He drew a grid. Across the top as column headers, he wrote the six purposes of the church—evangelism, worship, discipleship, compassion, community life, and global mission. Then he began to think of the various subcultures within his own congregation and wrote them down the left side as row headers.

	Evangelism	Worship	Discipleship	Compassion	Community Life	Global Mission
Children						
Youth						
University						
Adult						
Senior Adult						
Family						
Missions						
Small Groups						
Men						
Women						

When he was finished, Daniel decided the grid needed more work and more information. He jumped online and began to research missional organizing systems and discovered some items that led him to make a list of the characteristics of an effective missional structure:

- Missional: promotes accomplishment of the mission
- Visional: calls for vision to flow from the confluence of mission and culture
- Accountable: holds organization accountable to the mission and vision
- Directive: provides boundaries
- Flexible: allows for change and adaptability to fluctuating circumstances

- Manageable: allows leadership to practice accountability and follow-through
- Relevant: allows responsiveness to changing culture without losing God's purpose
- Teleological: moves people to God's desired goal (to become more Christlike)
- Efficient: not so large that it becomes cumbersome and slow to respond
- Participative: involves as many people as possible (laity in addition to clergy)
- Inclusive: all parts of the organization are in some way (directly or indirectly) represented at the leadership table
- Responsible: sets expectations and qualifications for leaders

Daniel thought this list would be great to remember and use as a checklist as his thoughts came to life. Then he smiled as he remembered his little girl, Caroline, and her favorite question these days: "Why?" She asked "why" about everything. Now it was his turn. *Why this image? What does this grid convey?*

Then it began to dawn on him. The point at which the purposes meet the subcultures is where missional, teleological, and practical put down roots and blossom into questions.

For example, thinking about the intersections of the youth subculture with the purposes, questions surface.

- What are the best ways to evangelize youth?
  - How do we get them involved in evangelizing their friends?
- What are the best ways we can engage youth in worship?

- ○ How do we teach them to worship in truth, authentically and meaningfully?
- ○ How do we help them see their place in intergenerational worship?
- What are the best ways to disciple students?
  - ○ How can we help them understand the way of Jesus in this world and what it means to be a follower of Jesus?
- How can we help youth understand the importance of compassionate ministry in our world?
  - ○ What can we do to engage them in meeting the needs of people around us and in our world?
  - ○ How can we help them practice compassion toward the disenfranchised, marginalized, and victimized?
- How do we help youth realize the importance of the community of faith?
  - ○ In a time when so many people underestimate and undervalue the importance of the church, how do we help them understand that the church is God's idea?
  - ○ Beyond understanding, how do we help them to commit to the church and to the mission God has for it in the world?
  - ○ How do we help them practice caring for others as they journey through life?

The answers to these questions would surface as the leaders who were passionate about each subculture met and prayed and grappled with each question. For now, Daniel knew his focus was on creating an organizational system that would allow for dialogue of this nature, giving rise to plans that would address each question.

There was something missing, however, from his organizational system. He realized the structure was a good missional grid, but it did not contain any reference to his governance board. What about the leadership of the congregation? Where should the governance board fit in?

As Daniel thought about leadership and particularly about what Jesus had to say about it, he recalled the story in Mark 10. Always one of his favorites, he remembered the audacity of James and John as they asked to sit on Jesus's left and right when Jesus became king. There are so many lessons in this story, but Daniel focused on one specific point Jesus made: Jesus turned leadership right-side-up when he said to all the disciples, "You know that among the gentiles those whom they recognize as their rulers lord it over them, and their great ones are tyrants over them. But it is not so among you; instead, whoever wishes to become great among you must be your servant, and whoever wishes to be first among you must be slave of all. For the Son of Man came not to be served but to serve and to give his life a ransom for many" (Mark 10:42b–45). With that concept in mind, Daniel added governance, or what he chose to call *administration*.

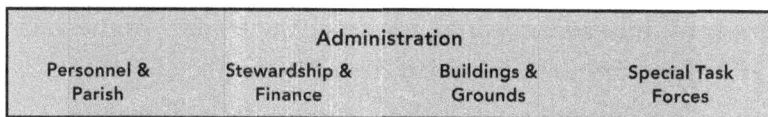

Administration			
Personnel & Parish	Stewardship & Finance	Buildings & Grounds	Special Task Forces

He thought about the various teams accountable to the governance board of their church.

The Personnel and Parish team oversaw personnel management policies and activities including job descriptions, compensation and benefits, and staff-parish relations. It was their role to serve as an advisory team to the lead pastor on sensitive interpersonal issues arising within the staff and/or congregation.

The Stewardship and Finance team had the fiduciary responsibility for overseeing the financial life of the church. The team was responsible for preparation and implementation of the church budget, ensuring accurate accounting for receipts and expenditures, and presenting regular finance reports to the church governance board.

The Buildings and Grounds team was responsible for caring for the facilities, grounds, and vehicles. They made recommendations to the governance board for action in these areas.

Special Task Forces were created from time to time based on specific goals or projects. Daniel remembered the construction task force developed to oversee the construction of their new facility a few years ago. When their task was complete, that team was dissolved.

Daniel now considered the question of where they fit on the missional organization grid. The reality of Jesus's words gave him an idea: put them on the bottom! Their job was to empower and enable the other ministries. They were the resources for the subcultures. They dealt with personnel, conflict, finances, facilities, and any other *equipping* kinds of things that would empower the leaders of the various ministries to accomplish their purposes.

"Put them on the bottom," he said to the raccoon.

	Evangelism	Worship	Discipleship	Compassion	Community Life	Global Missions
Children						
Youth						
University						
Adult						
Senior Adult						
Family						
Missions						
Small Groups						
Men						
Women						
Administration						
Personnel & Parish		Stewardship & Finance		Buildings & Grounds	Special Task Forces	

The raccoon? He had been so engulfed in his thoughts on organization that he had forgotten about the raccoon, but he realized he had addressed it just now because it was still there, outside, watching him from the other side of the creek. To Daniel's amazement, the little critter rubbed its hands together as if to say, *There. I've done my job.* The masked bandit gave Daniel what looked like a little smile and, with a click of the lips, darted off to the nearest trail, disappearing in the brush.

8

CAN YOU SEE IT?

Daniel woke up early the next morning. He thought about his answer to a question his wife, Erin, asked him every morning: "How did you sleep?" Although Erin was not with him on this adventure, she was never far from his heart and mind. "If Erin were here, I would tell her I didn't sleep well. Too many thoughts running through my head." What he usually did when he experienced this back home was to get up and start writing down the thoughts that raced through his mind. "I'll start there," he said, speaking out loud.

After a breakfast consisting of an egg sandwich, fruit, and coffee, Daniel began to make a list, which was typical of his methodology. First he wrote, *Beginning: Word of God.*

Then he thought, *No, that's not really correct. The beginning is with God. The starting point for everything is with the person of God. The triune God who is self-giving, holy love must be the ground from which everything else rises.*

Daniel looked around, grabbed a blank piece of paper, and drew some lines near the bottom, indicating the ground from which any creative thoughts might arise.

Triune God

Suddenly Daniel remembered what Dr. Darden had left on the counter in the kitchen before she had vanished—cups stacked in the shape of a pyramid. Had she tried to leave him a clue? Perhaps. He quickly started drawing a pyramid as he thought of all he had learned so far. The ground is God. On level 1 is the Word of the Lord—Scripture.

Scripture

Triune God

Thinking about Dr. Darden's presence reminded Daniel that all Scripture is viewed through various theological perspectives. Even the view of God as self-giving, holy love is a particular theological perspective. Systematic theology had helped Daniel appreciate consistent theological understandings. And it was somehow honest to admit the truth that we cannot really read Scripture without an underlying theological perspective. After all, it is called an *under-standing*. What we believe about God and his ways in the world shapes our understanding of the purposes of God for his people.

Daniel drew in the next level of the pyramid: theological understanding.

```
Theological
Understanding

Scripture
```

Triune God

"Don't forget about mission! Remember the *missio Dei*," Daniel reminded himself. Mission was key. In fact, Daniel realized, holding an organization accountable to its mission should probably be the number-one task of the leader of *any* organization. Mission is God's *what*—what God is all about in the world. The church's mission is to join God's mission in the world. Level 3 in the pyramid Daniel was slowly building was God's mission for the church.

```
Mission

Theological
Understanding

Scripture
```

Triune God

Recalling one of his conversations with Sam about specific tracks for the mission train to run on, he grouped these tracks together and thought of them as *purposes* for the church. The purposes flow from the mission but are more specific. Purposes are about *what* the church is to do in this world as it joins God's mission. Or, perhaps more accurately stated, they are what God wants to do in this world through the church. Daniel was able to locate himself in this layer. He was called to be the prophet, priest, and equipper for the purpose of leading the church into effective participation in the *missio Dei*. Level 4 was God's purposes for the church.

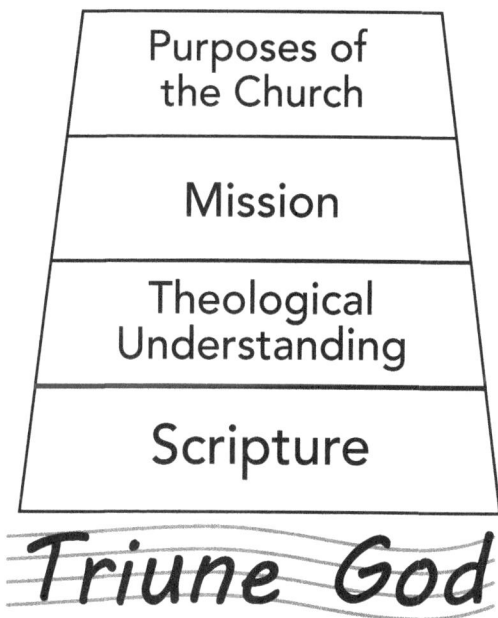

Next, Daniel remembered the missional ministry grid he had created the previous day. It was designed to bring the purposes of God together with the specific ministry context. In other words, God's purposes for the church express themselves within a specific local congregation and its culture. This is where the purposes begin to show up in that local context. This is also the place to formulate the right questions that in turn give rise to very specific ministries. Level 5 was ministry system/structure.

Ministry Structure/System
Purposes of the Church
Mission
Theological Understanding
Scripture

Triune God

Daniel pondered all this, staring off into the distant land of thought, looking at nothing in particular but everything in general. Something, or rather someone, caught his eye. There, on the highest peak—the one that looked now like the very pyramid he'd been contemplating—was a person walking up a trail.

What in the world? With all the characters Daniel had already encountered, he excitedly anticipated whom he might meet next. Another adventure today would be great!

Grabbing his binoculars and his backpack full of water bottles and power bars, he set out and soon spotted a trail that eventually would take him to a connecting trail that led up to the highest peak. Daniel said, "Well, let's get going. I've been wanting to see the view from that peak anyway, and now must be the time!"

As he hiked the first trail and then the connecting trail, he discovered a third trail that led up to the peak of what he was now calling Mount Pyramid. At the top, the trail opened onto a big, flat rock that allowed him to see in all directions. Daniel spoke his thoughts aloud. "Wow! This view from the top is fantastic!"

"It sure is!" said a deep voice from behind him.

Startled, Daniel turned around to see a man dressed in what appeared to be the uniform of a park ranger. He had wild, curly hair and a mustache that cascaded from the bottom of his nose to a cavernous dimple just above the point of his chin. That was some mustache!

"Hello," the man said. "My name is John Moore. I'm a conservationist from the adjoining park on the backside of this peak. I like to climb up here every so often just to survey the area. From here I can see where there may be trouble—fires, erosion, anyone who's lost, things like that. This vantage point gives me a great view of what is happening and any situations I need to address. I can see better how to manage the park from up here."

"It's a long way up here," Daniel said. "Farther than I thought when I started out."

"I know," said John. "You look up and think it's not that far to the peak—until you start the hike. This is the tallest mountain peak around here, and it has a great view of the valley below. I'm able to see for miles in every direction. By the way, I understand you've met my friend Sam. I run into him every now and then, and he always reminds me that he's the reason I come up here. It's my mission in life, he tells me. I saw him yesterday, and he wanted me to meet you up here and show you the view."

"It is quite a view," Daniel said. The thought occurred to Daniel, so he asked, "Since Sam sent you, did he want you to talk to me about anything in particular?"

"Sure did. He wanted me to meet you up here on this rocky mountaintop and talk to you about the way vision works."

"I know what I think of when I hear the word 'vision,'" Daniel said, "but I have no idea how you—and Sam—understand it. What is it?"

"Well, what do you think it is?"

"For me it's about mysterious, grand plans—you know, going to the holy mountain and coming down with a vision from the Almighty. At least, that's the way it often sounded to me."

"Hmm. We need to think through this in more practical, everyday, hands-on kinds of ways. Let's lose a little of the smoke and mirrors." John continued, "Vision has to do with seeing things clearly from a distance. Some people believe vision is seeing what others do not see. I'm not sure that exclusivity is necessary. In fact, it is better when others see it with you. The vision seems to be more powerful when it is shared."

"Do you mean when people buy in?" Daniel asked.

"Not really. *Buy-in* language is fine, but *participation* language may be better. When people are on the journey with you and together you see God's preferred future, you don't really need to worry about buy-in. Does that make sense? Plus, buy-in could imply the pastor is selling something as opposed to leading the people as a community to *participate*—or, maybe better still, *engage*—with God's mission."

John kept going before Daniel could answer. "A vision is a *consuming, passionate, compelling inner picture.* I like to say that vision is *seeing what is not yet as if it was already.* And, if you can do that with a group of people, the vision becomes even more compelling."

Thoughts now flowed through Daniel's mind. "Vision for a group of people, or for an organization, is about what the future could look like—a future that expresses the mission."

"Exactly. You're beginning to get your mind around it. Shared vision is vital to the life of any organization, and the church is no exception. In fact, consider Proverbs 29:18: 'Where there is no revelation, people cast off restraint; but blessed is the one who heeds wisdom's instruction'" (NIV). "Revelation is about vision. It is about God showing—revealing—his plan for the future."

"Some translations say *perish* instead of *cast off restraint,*" Daniel remembered.

"That's right," John said. "But think of the connection between the two. If you have no vision, no revelation from the Lord, no picture of what God wants to do in, through, and around you, then you cast off restraint. You don't discipline yourself toward particular goals and objectives. Anything goes. And that leads to death—death of the organization, of the church, even of people. Where there is no revelation, no vision, people lose focus, become undisciplined, and try anything or nothing—and they perish."

"Wow! Never thought of it quite like that," Daniel chimed in.

John said, "I like to call this the *fundamental imperative of vision*. It is imperative that I come up to this place routinely and look out to see. It is the same with you. Once you understand that vision flows from mission, you must stand on the peak of vision and look out to see what is needed."

Daniel had questions. "Do I simply think or imagine what the future could look like or what we need to be doing? I mean, how do I do this? What is the source of any worthwhile vision?"

"Go back to Proverbs 29:18. Revelation is *revealed*, obviously, but it is also received. The source of vision is ultimately the triune God. And God often reveals his preferred vision through the people around us. In fact, I like to say we *hear* a vision before we *see* a vision."

Hear a vision? That's odd language, Daniel thought, but kept it to himself.

John continued, "Listen to the gentle whispers of the Holy Spirit that often come through conversations with others. Listen for the dreams and ideas God is birthing in them. Stay attuned to the challenges people mention. It's almost like God takes a divine highlighter and highlights conversations and phrases, ideas and solutions, and even dreams people have for their church. He will bring those together and begin to form a picture of the not yet as if it was already."

"What if no one is dreaming about the church? What if no one in the church is passionate enough to recognize the possibilities for advancing the mission of God, let alone ponder solutions?" Daniel had to ask because this was one of his main points of burnout. He felt like he was trying to push a rope. It seemed to him that he was the only one who cared about the church engaging in meaningful ministry.

"You know, Daniel, one reason churches fail to have a vision for today and tomorrow is that they are living in the past. In fact, the prayer my pastor often prays with church leadership is, *'God give us people whose vision of the future is stronger than their memory of the past.'*"

"Now, that's a prayer worth praying!" Daniel said. "It takes the church together, and particularly church leadership—both lay and clergy—to speak into vision."

"Yes. Now you as pastor might need to go up on the mountain in order to pull together what you have heard and seen. And you might even do that with a small group of people. So I guess there is a mountain view involved in visioning." John smiled. "See, Daniel, when a church loses its sense of mission, it will naturally have no vision. God did not raise up the church to be a protector of tradition but to live out the life of Christ in the world. That takes vision!"

"I've had vision failure," Daniel said.

John nodded. "That's not uncommon at all! There are several issues that can cause vision failure:

- The vision is the pastor's vision only, not a shared vision.
- The vision is not clearly communicated.
- The vision does not include others.
- The vision lacks careful planning.
- The vision is poorly implemented.
- The vision is never reviewed and updated."

"I've made all those mistakes in my ministry," Daniel responded. "I think I'm beginning to *see* it, but I'm still struggling with the difference between mission and vision. I know there *is* a difference, but I'm not sure how to get my head around it."

"Again, not uncommon. You might think of the two like this: Vision is *mission in motion*. Vision is *applied mission*. Vision is *mission applied to today's culture* within the framework of our ministry structure. Vision stands at the intersection of mission and culture."

"What do you mean by the intersection of mission and culture?" asked Daniel.

"Use your imagination. Remember, its vision we're talking about. Imagination is part of visioning. Imagine a large avenue running north to south." John scratched a line representing an avenue in the dirt on the rock's surface.

Missio Dei Ave

"This is Missio Dei Avenue," John said. "It is crossed by culture streets. Imagine these run east and west. Think of some cultures in human history."

Hebrew Patriarchs

Greco-Roman

Missio Dei Ave

Middle Ages

Enlightenment

Modernity

Postmodern

Daniel responded, "Well, there was the culture of the Hebrew patriarchs. There was the culture of the Davidic kings and Babylon. Is this what you mean?"

"Yes! Keep going, particularly focusing on the cultures the church encountered."

Daniel listed some of the important cultural eras the church had encountered throughout history: "Greco-Roman, Middle Ages, Enlightenment, Modernity, Postmodernity. I could go on."

"That's enough for now. You'll see it," John said as he scratched in the dirt.

"Look at the intersection where Missio Dei Avenue meets Modernity Sreet. What was the vision? What did the church do? How did worship look? How did compassionate ministry look? How did it look to engage in discipleship or evangelism? How did the body of Christ come together in community? What form did global missions assume? Did that differ from how it looked in the Middle Ages? Did it differ from the Greco-Roman times of the early church?"

Daniel saw it. "Of course it did! In fact, how the church evangelized and discipled people was very different in the early church than in Modern times."

"That's right," John said. "But notice, Missio Dei Avenue did not change. God's mission to redeem, restore, recreate, and renew all creation didn't change. How it *looked* changed. How it was *enacted* changed. What the church specifically *did* changed. Its *methodology* changed. But the mission of God was constant."

Daniel replied, "Okay, so vision is seen on the corner of Missio Dei Avenue and Culture Street—whatever the culture might be. The specifics will look different, but they still must be in the vision."

"Exactly!"

"Okay," Daniel said, "but I'm still trying to get my head around mission and vision in terms of *action*. It seems to me, if I'm hearing you correctly, that mission is more stationary and vision is change-oriented. Am I on the right track?"

"You are," John replied, smiling. "Let me give you another metaphor. Think about a TV." Finding another place where dirt covered the rocky top of the mountain, John drew a box representing a TV. "Imagine this is a TV. The edge of the TV—the casing, if you prefer—is the mission."

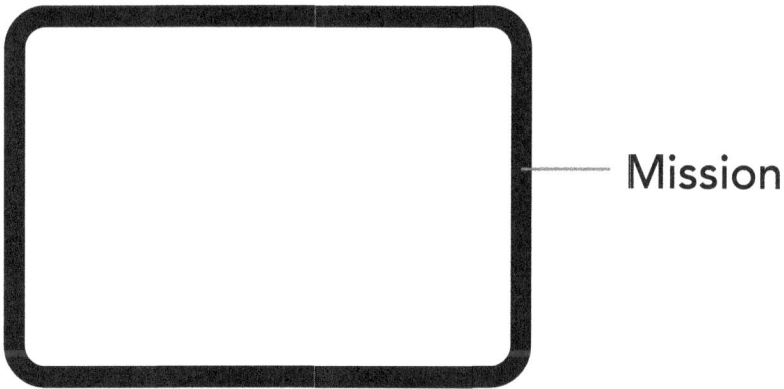

Mission

"Mission serves as the framework—this is what we are about. Mission also serves as the boundary—we don't go beyond this. This is our scope. And mission serves as a director—directing our attention, energy, and focus to the screen. If you sit down to watch TV and it is located on the west wall of the room, you don't face east to watch it. You direct your attention toward the TV—toward what is showing *inside* the frame. Are you with me so far?"

"I think I'm seeing it," Daniel replied.

John continued, "What is going on inside the frame is the vision. It is a moving picture. It is the scene unfolding. It is the story being told. It is ongoing, moving, changing, taking different shapes, following different story lines. Can you *see* it? It doesn't stop moving. If it stopped moving, we would call that *freezing up*, and it would tell us that something is wrong."

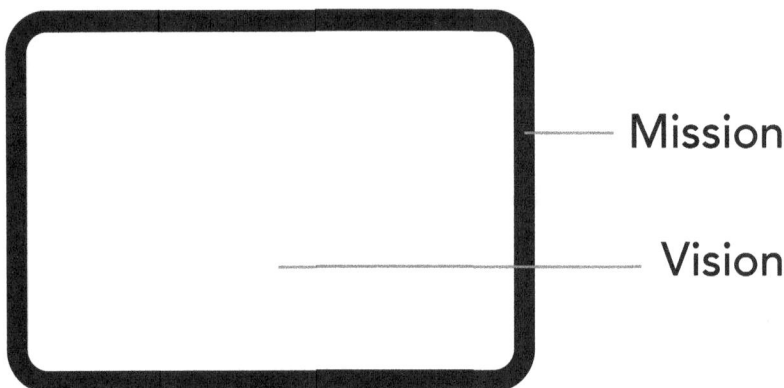

Mission

Vision

Daniel jumped in. "Yet many people in the church *want* the picture to freeze up—or even go back a few frames, then freeze."

"Yep. That's one of the vision killers," John reminded him. "But the picture is always moving. It's not static. The vision is about how the purposes look in real time being lived out continually. It really is mission in motion."

Daniel was seeing it now. "It's like how discipleship, for *years*, took place at the church facility in small classrooms on Sunday mornings. We called it Sunday school. But now, with the changes in postmodern culture, discipleship occurs in all kinds of ways and places—homes, restaurants, coffee shops, retreats, online in chat rooms and video conferencing!"

"The sky is not even the limit anymore, Daniel. Look out from this peak and see what you can and as far as you can. Isn't it beautiful!"

Daniel kept envisioning it. "It seems to me that a church should shape its specific ministries to its specific culture—that is, the way the purposes are *applied* to culture will and should vary. It probably would be difficult to lead people over age seventy in regular metaverse worship experiences."

John laughed. "That's right, Daniel. A local church must have a vision for joining God's mission that is specific for the culture in which that local church finds itself. What churches choose to do to evangelize and disciple will vary. *Whether* a church evangelizes and disciples should not be in question. How a church constructs worship gatherings that will create space and place for people to connect with the triune God will vary. But every church *should* be creating space and place for people to gather and worship."

Daniel said, "Finally, I think I got it!"

John continued, "Wait, there's more! There is another major aspect to this idea of vision. Think about your favorite movies. The movie has *scenes*, right? You could even think of them as events, or happenings. And those scenes take place in specific places at specific times. In essence, the events occur within a time frame or sequence."

Daniel interrupted as his own thoughts caught up. "You're talking about specific ministries being placed on a calendar."

"That's right, Daniel. It's not enough to simply see the vision of how the purposes work in the local culture. Good leaders—in fact, great leaders—move beyond this. Great leaders understand the necessity of holding the organization accountable to the vision, thus to the mission, thus to the Word of God, and thus to God himself. How many trails did you take to get up here, Daniel?"

"Three," Daniel replied.

"That's right, three different trails. Or, three different components to creating and sustaining vision. I like to call it the Vision Cycle. It is cyclical in nature, but over time it will result in a changing and relevant continual vision."

"What do you mean? Can you help me envision it?"

"Sure. The first component is establishing specific ministry objectives. These arise from the questions prompted by the missional ministry grid that you drew yesterday."

Specific Ministries/ Missional Objectives

Daniel jumped in and began formulating questions. "Okay, so things like, what is the most effective way to disciple women in our culture—or men, or parents with young children, or empty nesters? How can we most effectively engage children in compassionate ministry? What is the most effective way to help university students encounter God in worship? How do we engage youth in global missions?"

"I think you have the idea," John said. "You can ask tons of questions. In turn, the answers to those questions become your missional objectives. For example, one of the ways you might engage youth in compassionate ministry is take them on a mission trip to a different culture and have them serve kids and families. This ministry will address several of the purposes."

"Absolutely! Compassionate ministry, worship, community life, global missions, and discipleship! Oh, evangelism too!" Daniel said. "I could ask leaders who have a passion for these subcultures within the church to pray, brainstorm, and seek the will of God for specific ministries that would accomplish the purposes. I could have a ministry action team for each subculture, and each team would be responsible for creating the vision of ministry for its target audience. This could be fun!"

"Yeah, it is! But there is the second part that is sometimes not so fun—and that's accountability to the ministry objectives! That is a word that makes some people have a full-body shiver. Once a ministry objective is created, it must be given life. That means dates and budgets. As a leader, you can't hold someone accountable for a nebulous vision. The ministry object must be SMART. You know what that stands for, I'm sure: Specific, Measurable, Achievable, Result-oriented, Time-bound."

Specific
Identify exactly what you're going to do (i.e., a mission trip to a Caribbean island).

Measurable
How many are available to go? Also measure whether the trip actually happened.

Achievable
Can you actually do this? What's the cost? Do you have the human and financial resources to pull this off?

Result-oriented
Identify specific results you want to achieve through this ministry. This will also aid in measuring the effectiveness of the ministry.

Time-bound
Put it on the calendar. Put the dates you're going to start planning the event and all the steps that need to happen before you go—all the milestones that must be reached in order for the event to take place.

"Then," John said, "once all of that is identified, it is the role of the leader to hold people accountable to making sure it happens. That's often the tough part for leaders. People don't like to hold others accountable, nor do people always like to be *held* accountable! But any worthwhile vision requires accountability. This is true in every area of life, from sports to government to education to church. Everyone needs to be accountable."

Specific Ministries/ Missional Objectives

Accountability to Missional Objectives

Daniel's frustration moved to the front of his mind at that moment. "I think that's one of the reasons I'm here. I'm frustrated over people saying they will do something but never getting around to actually doing it. We get excited over a particular ministry event, but then it doesn't get done, or it's not done well. If I offer criticism, they may get mad and leave. People often talk a good game, but they don't produce on the field."

"I know. That is extremely frustrating and can lead to burnout!" John replied. "That's why you have to bring people into the conversation of mission and vision *early*. People have to help create all this. And accountability has to be agreed upon by everyone up front when they sign up to participate. If they want to participate, they need to be willing to be held accountable. Everyone needs to agree to be held accountable and be willing to hold others accountable. This is vital if vision is to become reality."

"You said there were three trails—I mean components—in the vision cycle," Daniel said.

"That's right. And the third one is analyzing the results. Once a ministry objective is accomplished, the leader responsible for it needs to ask honest questions regarding effectiveness. Did it accomplish what you hoped? Was it effective in meeting the purpose for which it was created? With the example of a mission trip to a Caribbean island, did the youth engage in compassionate ministry? Did it help them see the world in a more Christlike way? Did it deepen their understanding of God? Did they grow in their faith? Is there a greater sense of community among the youth now than before the trip?"

> ### Specific Ministries/
> ### Missional Objectives

> ### Accountability
> ### to Missional Objectives

> ### Analysis
> ### of Results

Daniel saw it. "Okay, so that's where it becomes a cycle. After the analysis, we would decide either to repeat the ministry objective or discard and replace it with a new one—or modify it to make it more effective. And this will keep the vision current. As culture shifts and changes, so can ministry objectives shift and change."

"You've got it now, Daniel." John moved to another patch of dirt and drew the entire vision cycle so Daniel could see it all laid out. "Start with specific ministry objectives. Move to accountability to ensure accomplishment of ministry objectives. Then conduct feedback and analysis to determine effectiveness, necessary changes, repetition, or elimination.

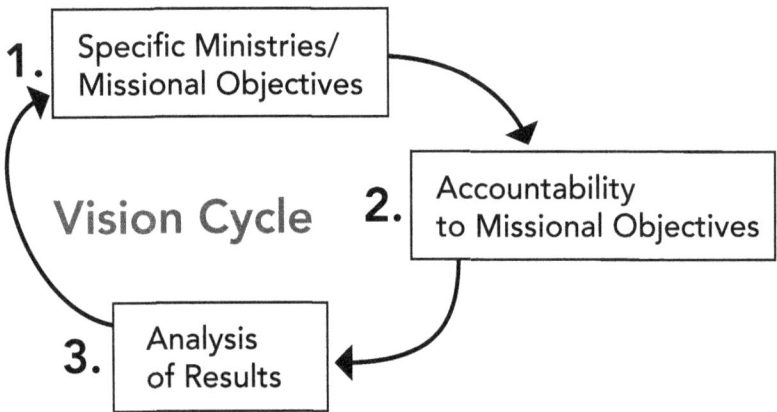

1. Specific Ministries/ Missional Objectives

Vision Cycle **2.** Accountability to Missional Objectives

3. Analysis of Results

Daniel remembered his pyramid. Here he was, on top of Mount Pyramid and thinking about the vision cycle. Now he could see it. Taking out his paper, he drew in the vision cycle right on top of his pyramid.

Then he turned to John and said, "You have really helped me see the vision about vision! I'm grateful Sam sent you my way." Daniel had half expected John to be gone already, but he was still there.

John said by way of farewell, "I've seen some issues I need to take care of." As John started off toward a trail that evidently led down to the park, Daniel heard him say, "You

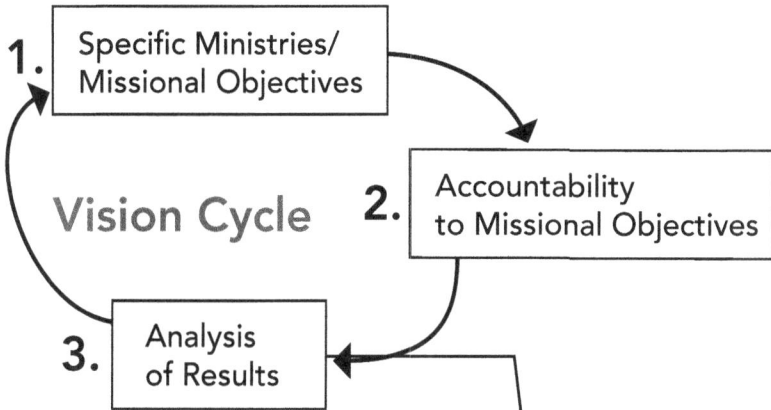

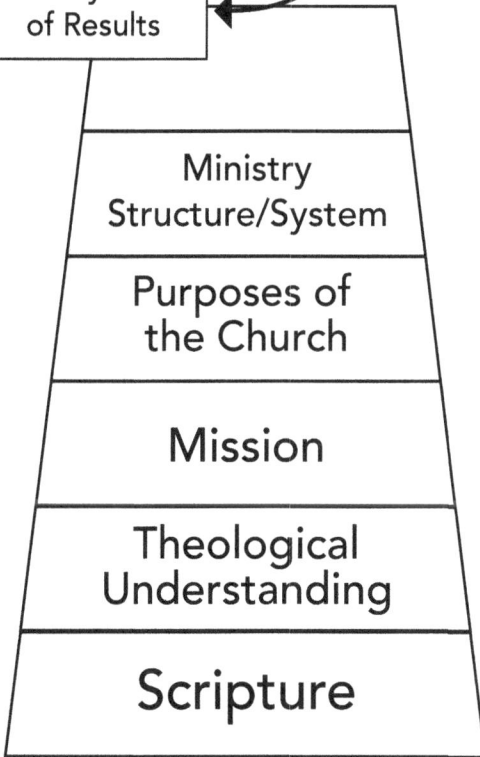

1. Specific Ministries/
Missional Objectives

Vision Cycle **2.** Accountability
to Missional Objectives

3. Analysis
of Results

Ministry
Structure/System

Purposes of
the Church

Mission

Theological
Understanding

Scripture

Triune God

know, if we cut a trail off to the west, people could better enjoy that area of the park. It would open an entirely new area for them. It's time to get it done."

Daniel said to himself, "It *is* time to get it done. See it, plan it, do it, analyze it. Get it done."

9

IT'S TIME TO CHANGE!

Daniel made his way back down the mountain, ideas and possibilities racing through his mind so fast he didn't notice the trail that branched off to the right that would've led him back to the cabin. After a few minutes his mind paused so he could figure out where he was on the hillside. Everything looked different. He had not been here before, and he wasn't even sure where *here* was.

How did he get here? Where *is* here? And, more importantly, how was he going to get back to the cabin?

"I'll just take a different route," he said aloud as he started down a trail to the left that he thought might circle back around at a lower point on the mountain. The trail was wide and pleasant at first, then began to narrow. The bushes started to cover the trail from his waist up, and he was having to push through them. Then it became covered from his knees all the way up over his head. It was obviously a small game trail and not a hiking trail at all.

Pushing through the brush like a football running back through a crowded offensive line, he broke into the open, almost falling, and found a beautiful clearing, complete with a tiny cabin, two apple trees, and a front porch. On the front porch in a rocking chair sat an older lady.

"Come on up and have a seat," she said to Daniel. I've been waiting for you to get here."

Who is this lady?

He'd not met her yet that he could recall. How could she have been waiting for him when he didn't even know he was going to end up here? But, after meeting Sam, Ed, and John, and after seeing his deceased theology professor, Dr. Darden, who knew who was next on his journey to renewal?

She pointed to an empty wooden rocking chair near her on the porch and directed Daniel to have a seat and relax. Then she was silent, almost to the point of awkwardness. She got up, walked into the little cabin, and brought out a cup of hot herbal tea. It had a little sugar in it, and it was delicious!

"Do you drink hot tea?" she asked.

"Not really," Daniel said. "I'm a coffee drinker when I want something hot, and I drink sweetened ice tea when I want something cold."

"Time for a change, then," she responded.

"You seemed to know I was coming your way. How?"

"Ed Griggs stopped by earlier and said you might be coming this way. He said, 'The boy is kinda lost, and he just might miss his trails.' His words, not mine."

"Well, he's right about that! The whole reason I'm on this mountain is to find some direction in life."

"You finding it yet?" the older lady probed.

"I'm beginning to, I think. I just had an amazing conversation with John Moore up on the peak of that mountain." He pointed to the highest peak. "You can see forever from that place! What a great spot to contemplate vision and see how the pieces fit together! I got a big-picture perspective from there. Now I need to do some work and strategize my way forward. By the way," Daniel continued, "I don't know your name."

"Let me introduce myself. I'm Susan Stanton, and I've had quite the journey in life! I lived a long time—born in 1901."

"What?" Daniel knew this dear lady could not be more than a hundred years old. No way! She appeared to be in her eighties, *maybe*. But thinking about Ed being an engineer from the early 1800s and Sam being an itinerant preacher from the late 1800s, he assumed Susan was just another apparition on this crazy journey.

Susan looked at Daniel and displayed a wry smile. "You're not sure I'm real, are you? Well, I'm as real as Sam, Ed, and John. Even as real as Dr. Darden. I've lived real life, my friend. I've been through so much change in my lifetime, it's hard to recall it all."

"Change?" Daniel responded. "That's one of the reasons I'm here. I desperately need things to change! I'm dying for change!"

"I've seen changes in my time, let me tell you!" Susan replied. "When I was born, my family rode in a wagon pulled by mules whenever we went to town on Saturday. It took us an hour each way. And when we went to town, there were stores that would not even let us enter—all because of the color of our skin. I saw the Great War come and go. And there were a lot of young men who left and never returned. I remember how people were crying their eyes out when the stock market crashed and they lost everything. The Great Depression put us all in the same boat called *Poverty*. But people still found a way to discriminate against us. But we got a car in those years. I don't know how my daddy did it, but one day he came home in one of those automobiles we'd seen on the roads they were building. From a mule-drawn wagon to a car—that's some kind of change. Another world war came along. Times were hard, but God saw us through it!"

Susan's eyes seemed to be focused far off into the distance as she recollected her past. She continued, "Women could vote now, but it was really hard for a Black woman to vote. We were still treated unfairly. But I remember the first time I heard Dr. Martin Luther King, Jr. preach." A smile creased her face, and a tear rolled down her cheek. "He had a dream. He had a dream to change the world. He had a vision—like one of those Old Testament prophets: 'Let justice roll down like waters and righteousness like an ever-flowing stream'" (see Amos 5:24). "You know, I heard him say that on the steps of the Lincoln Memorial. What a day! It was a time of great change!"

Daniel started to say something but thought better of it. He was lost in her memory at this point.

Susan kept going. "Why, I remember in July 1969 we watched on a TV—that was another change, by the way— we watched as Neil Armstrong walked on the moon. Think about it: in my lifetime I went from mules and wagons to automobiles to rockets to the moon! I went from hearing the news to reading the news to listening to the news all the way to seeing the news. Talk about changes! Oh my! And we could go anywhere now, even to the soda fountains in the drugstores."

She smiled at Daniel, and he knew what she meant.

Susan wasn't finished. "Here's the thing," she said. "We are not through changing. In fact, when a person is through changing, they are *through*! There are so many changes still needed. We must change the way we relate to each other as people. God does not discriminate; neither should we. God treats all people as equal; so should we. God loves everybody; so should we."

Susan was preaching now. Daniel heard an organ and choir in his head.

"God is leading us to the promised land. That means we're not *in* the promised land yet. That means change is not just something we have to tolerate; it is something we have to embrace. Change must become a way of life! God is a God of change!"

"Amen!" Daniel said before he thought.

Susan laughed. Daniel could see the deep joy on her face. "Yes, I've seen the changes in my lifetime, son. More change than I can even recall. You're going to see change too. You may see even more than me. The rate of change has sped up exponentially. Better buckle your seatbelt!"

Daniel was thinking now about change, and Susan seemed to read his mind. She said, "Yeah, you better buckle your seatbelt because not everyone embraces change. In fact, it seems like most people resist change."

"That's been true in my own ministry so far," Daniel said. "But why? Why do people resist change so much? I mean, at times it feels like people are *allergic* to change."

"That's true, Daniel. Most people do resist change, but they do so for some basic reasons. One reason is that *all change represents a loss of something.* When you're calling for change as a leader, that means something old must go in order for something new to come." Susan continued, "Also, *change challenges a person's sense of control.* Some people mistakenly believe they are in control. Now, sometimes they actually are. But change can challenge a person's sense of control, and that makes them very uncomfortable. It can even be seen as an attack on their own sense of self-worth."

Daniel thought of people who had resisted changes he'd suggested in the past and said, "I think some people resist change *in order to get even with an organization because of prior changes they didn't like.* I had that happen before in the church. A group of people didn't like a change the governance board made, so they decided to oppose the next change the board wanted to make—just to get even."

"That can happen," Susan said, "but sometimes people care deeply about the organization—the church, in your case—and resist because *they feel the organization they love is about to make a mistake.*"

"That makes sense," Daniel said. "In fact, leaders often want to label people who resist change as *bad,* but perhaps they just need more information and input in order to embrace change."

Susan said, "Resisting change can do more harm than good. Resisting change takes effort, and people can find more productive ways to spend their energy. Resisting change can be extremely divisive in a church, and in such cases nobody wins."

"That's right!" Daniel said. "You know, instead of focusing on the change itself, maybe it would be better if both the leadership and the people focused on the future. The change then becomes a byproduct of the path to the future. It becomes something you have to do so you can get where you want to go."

"Exactly, Daniel. A lot of people wait too long to make the necessary changes. They need to learn that waiting could be more harmful than changing. What's the cost to the organization if they *don't* make the changes? I remember when *The Wizard of Oz* was made into a movie. Movies! That was a change. In 1939, I was thirty-eight years old and found a way into the theater to see the classic featuring Dorothy, the Tin Man, the Scarecrow, and the Lion, who were all looking for change. The people under the rule of the wicked witch were also looking for change, but they lacked both courage and resources. A case could be made that the entire story was about change. On the road to change, the brave travelers encountered many barriers. Any worthwhile change will be met with barriers and obstacles. Think about your own life, Daniel. What changes have you encountered? Think about the lives of the churches you've served as pastor. What changes occurred there? Think about your family—any changes? Think about your culture. Has it changed in your lifetime?"

Daniel took a moment and thought about all the changes he'd experienced. Then he asked, "Is all change good?"

"No, not all change," Susan replied.

"Is change inevitable?" Daniel knew the answer before he asked the question, but Susan answered it anyway.

"Always! Remember what Heraclitus said, 'Change is the only constant.' Change is always hard work too. It might be helpful if you look into the stages of change. I could give you some wisdom on navigating change and helping your people through changes that need to be made. These are some of the different phases that occur when making a change." Susan listed the following for Daniel:

- Crisis/Need: The need for change can arise because of pain, or potential gain, or simply out of necessity due to other factors of change happening around you.

- Hard Work: This stage calls for research into possible solutions.
- Tough Decisions: You and the leadership team will sense a direction and begin to sense some optimism about the possibilities created from the needed change. But the decisions you must make will not usually be easy ones.
- Unexpected Pain: Often leadership teams think everyone should just jump on board right away, but that rarely happens. Leadership has spent time processing the ins and outs of the decision. The people often have not, so resistance may come unexpectedly, from quarters not yet considered by leadership. Many times an organization cannot grow without experiencing pain. The pushback can become a force to push the leadership team to more effective solutions. Or it might even help the people process the changes proposed.
- Joy and Integration: Changes are integrated, and life finds a new normal.

Daniel said, "So true! Then, after the joy and integration, you encounter new challenges and the need for *more* change."

"That's right! You got it! Change is the only constant. Learn to *em*brace it rather than simply brace it."

Daniel thought about his conversations thus far, about the foundation for ministry, the *missio Dei*, and the purposes God has for the church. He remembered the concepts of ministry systems and how the idea of a vision cycle would create a continual sense of change. He said, "When your mission meets your target audience, it often results in a change in methodology."

Susan knew how life worked, so she added, "Be careful because changes in methodology can be in conflict with your funding sources—particularly if your funding sources are not in unity with your mission and target audience."

Daniel said, "That's why it is so important to get people on board with the mission of God in the world and how God raised up the church to be the instrument through which he plays his redemption songs. Being obsessed with the *missio Dei* is vital!"

Susan adjusted Daniel's language a little. "Being *possessed* by God—as in, Jesus is Lord of all—is the vital piece. If Jesus is truly Lord of all in the lives of people, then you don't have to worry about people being all in on God's mission in the world. They will be all in because Jesus is all in! You know, Daniel, some people believe that when problems arise from making changes, it means the change was bad. But that's not true. Major change cannot possibly be problem-free."

"I've been there," Daniel replied. "Plus, some people even think it will help if they get really upset and fight it. All they end up doing is embarrassing themselves when their attitude becomes unChristlike. It's okay to question changes. But it's never okay to be unChristlike."

Now Susan said, "Amen!" She added, "I wish people could learn to be agents of positive change. They could if they would be *open* to change. Plus, they need the empowerment of the Holy Spirit to help them control their attitude *toward* change. Some people just start each day as if they sucked on sour grapes all night long."

Daniel laughed. "I know what you mean. I wish people would be a little more tolerant and gracious with leaders. Leaders definitely make mistakes!"

"One thing I learned from the life of Dr. Martin Luther King, Jr. is that we need to invent the future instead of trying to redesign the past. I don't think he ever said it that way, but that is exactly how he lived. He pointed us toward a preferred future that was all about change."

That prompted Daniel to say, "That's exactly what God does too. God is an agent of change. In fact, he is the ultimate agent of change. Sometimes we call it transformation. But it is really all about change."

"Change can also be known as *innovation*," Susan said. "We live in a world of innovation. From smart devices to satellites, from solar power to electric cars, we are a world of innovators. I've seen so much in my lifetime! Innovation is what change really is. God is the ultimate innovator."

Daniel replied, "I've had people ask me why we should change, and they quote Hebrews 13:8: 'Jesus Christ is the same yesterday and today and forever.' Or they quote the prophet Malachi, 'For I the LORD do not change'" (Malachi 3:6).

Susan chimed in with her knowledge of the Bible. "Malachi 3:6 is set in a context of grace and judgment. Also, the word "change" in this context means "duplicity" or "variations." In essence, God's nature is the same. His love, his holiness, his characteristics will never change. He is and will forever be self-giving, holy love. But to think God never changes *how* he works through his people in his world would be inconsistent with what we know to be true. I would tell them to read all through the Bible and ask them if they found that God always did the same thing in every situation. I don't think so. *God is an innovator*, Daniel. The first verb in the first verse in the first book of the Bible is *bara*—'created.' God is a God of innovation! God told Isaiah in Isaiah 43:18–19: 'Do not remember the former things or consider the things of old. I am about to do a new thing; now it springs forth; do you not perceive it? I will make a way in the wilderness and rivers in the desert.'"

"Jesus was—or is—an innovator too," Daniel added. "He even offered a new covenant. Plus, he said in Matthew 18:3–4, 'Truly I tell you, unless you change and become like children, you will never enter the kingdom of heaven.' Jesus was teaching his disciples about their attitude because the disciples were maybe thinking more of themselves than they ought. In fact, one of them had just come to Jesus and asked who was the greatest in the kingdom of heaven. Jesus told them they needed to change. Jesus was all about change—or, better yet, innovation."

"You know, Daniel, most of our difficulty with change comes from our attitudes rather than from our actions."

As Daniel fixated on that last statement, Susan completed the Trinitarian thought. "The Holy Spirit is also an agent of change. Remember Romans 12:2: 'Do not be conformed to this age, but be transformed'—a word that indicates continual change—'by the renewing of the mind, so that you may discern what is the will of God—what is good and acceptable and perfect.' Or what about Paul's words in 2 Corinthians 5:17? 'So if anyone is in Christ, there is a new creation: everything old has passed away; look, new things have come into being!'"

Susan got up from her rocking chair suddenly and walked into the kitchen, picking up Daniel's empty mug of hot tea as she passed. Daniel sat there gently rocking while he contemplated the conversation on change. *Yeah, this could be tough to pull off. But the challenges intrinsic to the changes do not minimize the necessity of innovation. Some-*

thing has to change. And, by God's grace and empowerment, it will!

Susan returned with a bottle of water. "You might want to take this back to your cabin. You have a long way to go, but you'll get there. I hope this will help."

"Oh, this will definitely help! Your wisdom and counsel on change are the dose of reality I needed at this moment. It'll help me plan more effectively as I involve more people in the process. Oh, and the water will help too. I'm just about empty!"

Daniel turned to wave goodbye as he approached the trailhead, and he saw Susan still on the porch, rearranging the furniture.

10

WE'RE IN THIS TOGETHER

The hike back to his cabin provided Daniel with different scenery than he had experienced so far. There were twists and turns through creeks and streams, fallen trees to climb over, and a few huge boulders to skirt around. But the overlooks were fantastic!

Back in his cabin with a cup of coffee in his hand, Daniel began to reflect on what he'd learned so far. Ideas bombarded his mind like nuclear fusion, and there was an energy being released in him. He was beginning to feel hopeful as he thought of returning home. He really wanted to return energized and inspired. He deeply desired a renewed sense of missional excitement. He needed a holy passion that would follow what he now identified as holy discontent. It was growing!

There was still something missing, however. He felt like things were still a little scattered and chaotic. How could he pull everything together?

Daniel pulled out his sketch of the pyramid—what he found himself calling the Missional Ministry Pyramid.

```
┌─────────────────────────┐
│         Ministry        │
│      Structure/System   │
├─────────────────────────┤
│       Purposes of       │
│        the Church       │
├─────────────────────────┤
│          Mission        │
├─────────────────────────┤
│       Theological       │
│      Understanding      │
├─────────────────────────┤
│         Scripture       │
└─────────────────────────┘
        Triune God
```

Then, thinking about that day's conversations, he added the Vision Cycle.

Daniel picked up his laptop and begin to write summary statements about each level, starting at the bottom and working his way up.

Triune God: God the Father, Son, and Holy Spirit is the foundation of everything.

Scripture: Reveals the character and mission of God in the world as well as God's authority.

Theological Understanding: An honest admission of the lens through which we read Scripture, and a call for consistency.

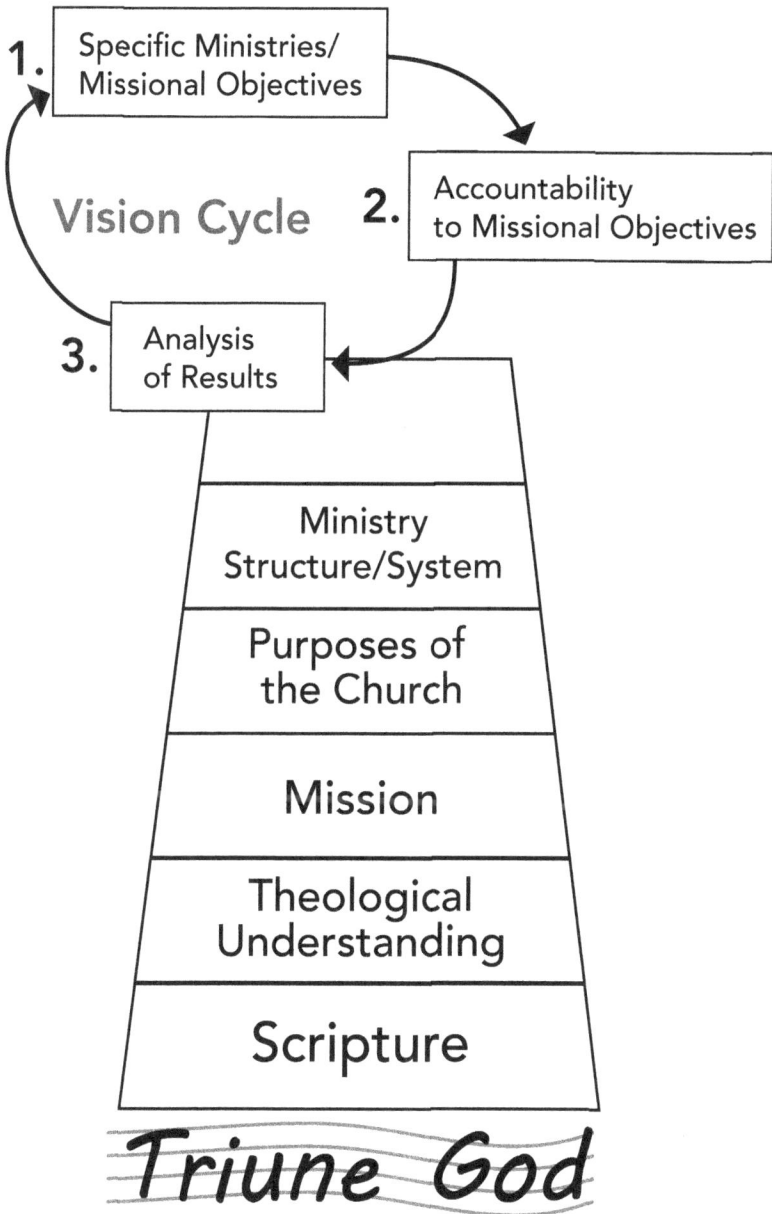

1. Specific Ministries/ Missional Objectives

2. Accountability to Missional Objectives

Vision Cycle

3. Analysis of Results

Ministry Structure/System

Purposes of the Church

Mission

Theological Understanding

Scripture

Triune God

Mission: An understanding of the *missio Dei* and God's intention to redeem, restore, and reconcile all creation to himself.

Purposes of the Church: The categorical ways that God desires to use the church to accomplish his mission.

Ministry Structure/System: The way the church organizes itself in order to most effectively join God's mission in the world.

Vision: Continual actions and expressions of God's mission and purposes within specific cultural contexts; how the mission and purposes look in everyday life.

Vision Cycle: A method of establishing specific vision actions, holding the church accountable to do what it plans to do, and analyzing the ministries for effectiveness.

Looking over his work, Daniel asked himself pointed questions: "Can this work? Can I do this? What role does my staff need to play? What about the governance board? What about the entire church? I mean, this looks good, but how can I get it done?"

Daniel silently prayed for wisdom, asking God to teach him how to do it. His desire to be effective for the mission of God in the world was overwhelming. It always had been. He knew he was called to this life of ministry, but the sense of defeat had admittedly gotten the best of him at times. But here, in this place, away from distractions, where he could think and pray, he'd been able to embrace his sense of calling once more.

Daniel glanced around the cabin. He hadn't noticed before, but now this place reminded him of a similar place where he and his family liked to go with his parents. He thought about the conversations he'd had with his mom and dad, who were both ministers. A lot of ministerial wisdom had been passed along in those conversations. Daniel also thought about how he often was the one to start those conversations. *"Let me get your input on an idea I have."* He smiled as he thought about how they always had an opinion. Multiple times through the years, whenever he discussed ministry challenges with his parents, they mentioned two items in particular: involvement and questions. Involvement and questions. The phrase was like a mantra.

Mom loved to say, "Get people involved in the work of the church; people rarely criticize their own work."

Dad would add, "The more people you have involved, the more people will support and work to make the ministry effective. They want everything with their name on it to succeed."

Then Mom would remind him, "Ask questions. Put everything in the form of questions. Get people thinking. Let them follow their own logic trails and see where they lead. Ask them how they feel. What do their instincts tell them? Questions are the keys to unlocking the dreams of people's hearts."

The ideas of involvement and questions ran headlong into the need for action. *How can I organize this in a way that gets people involved and frees them to be creative on the right missional objectives?*

Daniel looked at his phone as a notification appeared on the screen. It was a newsflash about his favorite football team. Daniel loved football. It was an intense hobby to keep up with recruiting, coaching, players, injury reports, and even prognostications about the success of the team against their next opponent. "The Tigers QB Room Is the Best Ever," the headline declared.

All of it came together at once in Daniel's mind: TEAMS!

Teams involve more people.

Teams create a common goal.

Teams allow for multiple perspectives.

Teams utilize a wider range of skillsets.

Teams increase a sense of community and belonging.

Teams increase transparency.

Teams apply accountability.

Teams allow people in a volunteer organization to take responsibility for bite-sized pieces of ministry.

There were so many more advantages created by using teams, but the ones he immediately thought of were enough to convince him that a team approach was the way to go. Football became the metaphor because, within a football team, there were multiple different kinds of smaller teams: defensive line, linebackers, defensive backs, offensive line, tight ends, wide receivers, running backs, quarterbacks. And that didn't even include special teams.

	Evangelism	Worship	Discipleship	Compassion	Community Life	Global Missions
Children						
Youth						
University						
Adult						
Senior Adult						
Family						
Missions						
Small Groups						
Men						
Women						
Administration						
Personnel & Parish		Stewardship & Finance		Buildings & Grounds		Special Task Forces

Daniel reached for the paper containing his missional ministry grid.

"Teams," he said. "What about calling them Missional Action Teams—or MATs, for short?" He smiled as he thought about how people loved acronyms.

His earlier thought about questions arising at the points of intersection on the grid came back to him. This time, though, the MAT needed to be the one asking the questions. The children's MAT, for example, could ask things like:

- What are the best ways to evangelize our children?
  - How do we get them involved in evangelizing their friends?
  - What can we do to help them come to faith and bring others to faith in Christ?
- What are the best ways we can engage our children in worship, particularly in ways they can understand and connect with God?
  - How do we help them see their place in intergenerational worship?
- What are the best ways or ideas for discipling our children?
  - How can we help them understand the way of Jesus in this world and what it means to be a follower of Jesus?
  - How do we involve their families in their discipleship?
- How can we help our children understand the importance of compassionate ministry in our world?
  - What can we do to engage them in meeting the needs of the people around us and in our world?

- How can we help them practice compassion toward the disenfranchised, marginalized, and victimized in our world?
- How do we help our children realize the importance of church?
  - In a time when there are so many activities competing for their attention and involvement, how do we help them understand that the church is God's idea?
  - And, beyond understanding, how do we help them to commit to the church and to the mission God has for it in the world?
  - How do we help them practice caring for others as they journey through life?

It's all about asking the right questions, Daniel thought. The answers would have differed at each of the churches he had served as pastor. Each church was in a slightly different culture, and their context-specific answers would have varied. However, the questions remained the same and would have generated meaningful missional ministry in all contexts.

Every subculture within the church could have a MAT. Each MAT could be composed of someone who would be responsible for one of the purposes. In some cases with fewer volunteers, a team member might be responsible for more than one purpose. The ideal was one, though. A Children's MAT could be composed of:

Team Leader: Responsible for leading/facilitating the meetings, holding people accountable to the mission and task they agreed to do.

Evangelism Leader: Responsible for leading the ways in which children are offered the opportunity to enter into a faith relationship with Jesus as well as leading any attempts to help children introduce their friends to Jesus through the church or other ministries.

Worship Leader: Responsible for ministries intended to help children encounter Christ in acts of worship.

Discipleship Leader: Responsible for curriculum and resources designed to teach children the way and ethics of the kingdom of Christ, understanding that following Jesus himself is the underlying goal.

Compassionate Ministry Leader: Responsible for creating opportunities for children to be involved in meeting the needs of others, thinking particularly of food, clothes, and shelter.

Community Life Leader: Responsible for creating opportunities for children to build relationships with one another.

Global Missions Leader: Responsible for engaging the children in reaching other cultures around the world through learning, sharing, and praying.

These team members would work together and then recruit as many people as necessary to be involved in each ministry. The MAT could meet annually to plan the year's missional objectives, allowing them to create dates, budgets, communication pieces, and anything else needed in advance to make the ministry effective. The team could also meet monthly to manage the details, allowing for real-time accountability and any adjustments that might need to be made due to changing circumstances.

The ideas expanded in Daniel's mind, and he gave voice to his thoughts. "This could be replicated with every subculture, every ministry focus in the church. There would be room for hundreds of people to be involved! They would all be asking the right questions. It would be flexible and consistently relevant to the church's culture and context. People would be engaged in doing the work of the kingdom. People could find real meaning and fulfillment in the mission of God in the world. Lives would be changed and transformed. Families could be restored. Generations would be positively impacted by this approach!"

Daniel paused and gave himself time to let all his thoughts sink in. Having energy for the mission was not his issue right now. Getting to it fast enough was his new challenge.

Then a very real question entered his mind: *Can just anyone serve with or on a MAT, or do there need to be qualifications for leadership? If so, what qualifications are necessary?* Again, Daniel started thinking in questions.

Do they need to be Christian already?

Do they need to be members of the local church?

Do they need to tithe?

Do they need to be in alignment theologically with the church?

Do they need to indicate willingness to be held accountable for the ministry they agree to serve?

Do they need a background check?

Daniel debated with himself. "Not everyone needs all this. But it would be negligent not to address these qualifications in some ministry roles." What he needed was a rule of thumb that would guide qualification decisions. They could not all be the same for every role. Perhaps the answer was: *As the leadership responsibility increases, the leadership commitment increases. As goes the leadership responsibility, so go the leadership qualifications.*

Daniel realized, *I don't need to decide this by myself. I need to involve the governance board in this decision. I can bring the issues to the table, and together we can create a list of qualifications for various levels of ministry involvement.*

Daniel's thoughts returned to the grid and the MATs, and he now knew that the compilation of the answers created by each MAT would together form the vision. He could create a document that contained every MAT's missional objectives, complete with dates and other necessary information. Each missional objective would have a budget to be approved (or adjusted then approved) by the finance team, thus allowing for good stewardship.

His responsibility, Daniel realized, would be to hold the leaders of the MATs accountable. Since he had a youth pastor, he could hold the youth pastor accountable for all MATs that may be developed in the youth department.

Daniel saw the potential for exponential growth in the engagement of people in the life of the church. He could host leadership development days, in which everyone involved in ministry could sharpen their skills and increase their potential for effectiveness.

"This could be great!"

Daniel took a deep breath and realized the sense of relief overtaking him. What a day! Ideas had been birthed for mission, vision, vision cycle, ministry grid, MATs, and even leadership development.

It was time for supper, and Daniel realized he was very hungry. Somehow he had totally missed lunch. In fact, he'd only had half a power bar on the trail that day. Knowing this was his last night in the cabin, he had saved a steak to grill. Steak, butter beans, a baked sweet potato, some salad, and cowboy peach cobbler. He would enjoy eating tonight!

11

BENEDICTION

The next morning, Daniel awoke moments before the sunrise. The morning was once again spectacular. As he did on his first morning at the cabin, he walked out on the front porch and witnessed the miracle of sunrise. He remembered how, on the first morning, the sunrise felt symbolic of this trip. Now that symbolism was affirmed. "This is going to be a new day," he said.

After breakfast, Daniel decided to go on one last, short hike before loading the car for the return trip. He felt like this trip had been productive, and he really believed he would be able to implement his newfound approach.

Spotting a previously unchosen trail, he smiled as he thought about Susan. *Change is good. I haven't walked this trail before. It just might be fun!*

The scenery on the trail was spectacular. There were overlooks that offered incredible views of far-off, blue mountains. He crossed a few streams, pausing to enjoy the sounds of water bouncing over ancient rocks. The trees were always fascinating. Fir, pine, oak, hickory, maple—he couldn't name them all, but he did enjoy them.

Daniel had been hiking for about twenty minutes when a sound made its way into his consciousness. Music . . . music that was familiar . . . and it was coming from just up the trail. When he went a little farther, the trail abruptly opened into a clearing, free from the density of the trees through which he had just passed. There, in the middle of the clearing, Daniel located the source of the music. It was a little white country church, built in an old-fashioned style. He approached the entrance, walked through the quaint double doors propped open for anyone and everyone, and found himself in a small vestibule.

Double swinging doors led from the foyer right into a sanctuary with nine rows of oak pews, filled with people, on each side of a center aisle. Daniel looked up and admired the dark-stained, exposed wooden beams supporting a tongue-and-groove decking that formed the whitewashed ceiling. It made a beautiful combination. Down each side of the sanctuary were windows filled with old, leaded stained glass, five on each side, individually depicting a traditional scene: creation, incarnation, Jesus teaching on the hillside, Jesus healing a disabled man, Jesus holding a lost lamb, baptism, the Lord's Supper, three crosses, an empty tomb, and Jesus returning from the heavens. It was worshipful and beautiful!

Letting his eyes move to the front, Daniel saw a little wooden pulpit with two chairs that looked like miniature thrones on each side and slightly behind it. A piano sat on the left of the platform and an organ on the right. And in the center behind the small choir loft was a simple, wooden cross.

The entire scene drew Daniel in. Finding an empty spot on the right side, he sat down and started singing with the people.

Over there was Sam. Daniel thought, *I bet Sam's preaching today. There's Ed—I didn't know he played the piano!* Dr. Darden smiled as she looked his way. Daniel noticed John sitting near the back, presumably in case he needed to slip out and take care of a problem in the park. Daniel heard the most beautiful voice to his left and saw Susan singing with a passion born deep in her soul.

The music ended. Sam stepped up, wearing his frock coat, and began to preach with passion about the *need* for passion. He railed against the encroachment of apathy upon the soul. "Apathy is a disease that slowly suffocates the heart, leaving us useless and irrelevant before the Lord," Sam proclaimed. "We need the fire of the Holy Spirit to burn within us!" Sam poured out his heart for Jesus and declared his passion for all people to enter into a life-transforming relationship with Christ.

Daniel sensed the Spirit of God moving in his own heart. In fact, it was as if the Holy Spirit were directing his eyes to the symbols in the little chapel while letting the words of the sermon serve as commentary for each symbol. Daniel began to see the merger of the message about passion for Jesus with the symbols of God's passion for his creation depicted in the stained-glass windows. Again, his eyes followed the path of the windows, which in turn led him to the simple wooden cross at the front. Everything—from the sermon to the stained-glass windows—announced love, compassion, mercy, forgiveness, redemption, freedom, and mission.

Daniel realized he could not lead the church into missional effectiveness without the fire of the Holy Spirit in his own heart. What he needed most was for God to fan into flame the embers that now burned in his heart. As tears filled his eyes, Daniel heard himself praying out loud for God to set his own soul on fire with the fire of the Holy Spirit that could not be quenched.

At the close of the sermon, Sam gave an opportunity for any who wanted to come and pray for wisdom and strength from the Spirit of God. Daniel went forward and knelt at the little wooden altar, knowing that any effectiveness resulting from this trip would be all God's doing and all God's glory. As he began to pray and pour his heart out to God, Daniel realized he was not alone. He was surrounded by a cloud of witnesses named Sam, Ed, Anne, John, and Susan. Somehow, he knew there were more than these praying for him and lifting him up. He remembered in that moment that Jesus himself was intervening for him. What a moment!

The benediction was pronounced, and church concluded. Feeling a sense of both relief and renewal, Daniel thanked his friends and walked down the few steps into the front yard of the little church. The last person to speak to him was Sam. "What a great word from the Lord today, Sam," Daniel said.

"Thank you, Daniel. Everything good that comes from the foolishness of preaching is from the Lord." Daniel turned toward the trail, and Sam said, "Daniel, you know you can't do this alone."

"I know. But now I also know the Holy Spirit has revived me, and with God, all things are possible."

"That's true," Sam said, "and there is something else extremely important."

Daniel paused, trying to figure out where Sam was going with this.

Sam said, "You can't do this alone. What I mean is that your people—the leaders in the church you serve, everyone who considers the church their community of faith—they must also share the passion! The passion for the kingdom of Christ to come and for God's will to be done on earth as it is in heaven must burn in every Christ follower's heart. You can't do it alone!"

"How do I help my people feel this passion?"

"How did you reach this place?" Sam asked.

"Well, I came up here, got away from everything . . ." Daniel's thoughts trailed off.

"That's right. In other words, you intentionally sought the presence of God for direction and guidance in your life and in the world around you. You need to lead your people into deep prayer. Include fasting. Lead them into an authentic quest for the heart of God. Lead them to pray."

Daniel responded, "I've preached on prayer, taught about prayer, called people to pray, and sent out prayer lists. But I need to build prayer itself into the life of the church. There must be opportunities for us to seek God and to take our needs, our families, our friends, our neighbors, our communities, and our nation before the Lord in prayer. We can start with prayer."

"Prayer is not just *a* starting placing; it is *the* starting place. And prayer is not a one-off event; it must be woven into the fabric of church life. See, Daniel, you cannot transform the world; you can't even transform yourself. You cannot save the world; you can't even save yourself. God, through continual prayer, will bring transformation and salvation to you, to his church, and to his world." Sam turned and walked back toward the little chapel.

Daniel stood in silence for a moment. He breathed a prayer asking God to go before him, preparing the hearts of the people to embrace the mission of God. Daniel said to himself, "Prayer! I'll start with prayer! I'll continue with prayer!"

Daniel hiked back to the cabin, loaded up his car, and thought, *What a trip! I knew I needed to get away. But what I found was a way to move forward in the calling God has renewed in my life.* This place and time had become precious to him. It was a watershed moment. Consequently, there was a strange mixture of sadness and excitement, with a lot of determination and humility thrown in for good measure.

"Time to go to work!" Daniel declared in an attempt to move toward the car.

As Daniel drove away from the cabin, he glimpsed one more of his friends—the little raccoon. "I declare, that little rascal looks like he's smiling."

APPENDIX A

■——■

Pastor as Prophet, Priest, and Equipper (Chapter 5)

Prophet

- Stands apart from the authority of the community and communicates the passion of God in judgment against evil, the call to repentance, and the invitation to renewed covenantal relationship
- Feels the passion of God in the divine emotions of suffering with the disobedient
- Challenges the people to be the faithful people of God; faithful to the covenant
- Proclaims the gospel—sometimes confrontationally

Priest

- Finds definition and function *only in community*
- Pastoral calling
- Visitation of the sick
- Informal pastoral counseling
- Bearing of the congregants' burdens
- Mediator (Christ's representative to the people of God)
- Helps the community understand their identity
- Helps establish community, intimacy, relationship, and mutual feeling

- Deals with conflict
- Promotes unity
- Calls the people to worship

Equipper
- Finds definition within the community of faith
- The heart of God calling people and equipping people to employ their talents is expressed in this role (see Ephesians 4:11–16)
- Prepares disciples to be priests to the world
- Empowerment
- Organization and administration
- Leadership
- Visionary
- Lay ministry

APPENDIX B

■━━■

Sample Mission Statement (Chapter 6)

| Grace
Community Church | Mission |

The mission of Grace Community Church is to ...
... join God's mission to share the kingdom of Christ with all people

Love God. Love People. Serve the World.

To this end, GCC engages in ...
Worship (Mt. 22:37; Dt. 6:5)
Discipleship (Mt. 28:19-20)
Compassionate Ministry (Mt. 22:39; Lev. 19:18)
Community Life (Mt. 28:19)
Evangelism (Mt. 28:19-20; Gen. 12:1-3)
Global Missions (Matthew 28:19-20; Acts 1:8)

Vision Statements ...
We will **worship** Christ in the spirit of truth and in the beauty of holiness
We will meet together in order to grow as **disciples** in the grace and knowledge of our Lord Jesus Christ
We will help others locally and globally through **compassionate ministries** and social justice
We will live as a **community**, building eternal friendships and drawing strength and encouragement from one another
We will intentionally **share our faith** with others locally and globally, inviting them to follow Jesus
We will partner with other followers of Jesus to advance his kingdom **around the globe**
We will actively engage in **caring for all creation**

Core Values ...

Grace	Transformation
Christlikeness/Holiness	Boundaries
Spiritual Servant Leadership	People
Authenticity	Faith
Stewardship of All Resources	Unconditional Love
Accountable Relationships	Celebrating Life Together

APPENDIX C

■———————■

Excursus: Toward a Theology of Organization

Organization Structure: Why Does It Even Matter?
Some make the case that the church is not an organization but an organism. In reality it is both. It is an organized organism, and as such, attention must be given to the organizational aspects of the organism.[1]

Organizations are complicated. The old style of top-down leadership is rarely effective in this age. Quantum physics, synergism, and multi-dimensional relationships all play a major role in the understanding of organizations. The move has been to envision organizations in a three-dimensional fashion as opposed to a two-dimensional way.[2] Two-dimensional organization reflects the old system—top down and horizontal levels. Three-dimensional organization occurs when all parts of the organization relate to one another in various ways, at various times, for various purposes. An organizational system must be designed properly if the organization is to be effective.[3]

---

1. Dwight M. Gunter II, *Leading a Church through Organizational Transition within a Changing Vision*, Dissertation (April 5, 2000), 21.

2. Gunter, *Leading a Church through Organizational Transition*, 21.

3. Gunter, *Leading a Church through Organizational Transition*, 22.

Mission and Vision

Organizations must begin with a mission. A clearly articulated mission will serve as a foundation for building an organizational system. The mission answers the simple question of *why we are here*. It addresses the reason of existence and the focus of the organization. The mission should be used to hold the organization accountable. The mission is the compass for deciding the course of action in a changing world and the plumb line used for measuring results. The mission is the framework for determining what training the leadership needs. It is the bottom line of the organization. Without mission, there is no meaning.[4]

Vision is separate from mission and flows *from* the mission. Mission is the picture frame—the boundary. Vision is the picture. Mission is the television equipment; vision is the movie. Vision is what is *seen*. It is how the organization looks today when it is accomplishing its mission. Vision is mission applied to contemporary culture.

A mission statement can start as follows: *It is the mission of this organization to . . .*

A vision statement can look more like this: *The mission of this organization is being accomplished when. . .*

Mission is a broad summary. Vision is a specific game plan.[5]

An organizational system is needed that focuses people's attention on the mission and vision. There simply must be a clear mission and vision if organizations want to achieve their objectives. The *main thing* must be guarded as

---

4. Gunter, *Leading a Church through Organizational Transition*, 22.

5. Gunter, *Leading a Church through Organizational Transition*, 22–23.

the *main thing*. The system should place the right perspective in front of people. Of course, it is up to each individual to choose to see it.

Enabling Progress

An organizational system is needed that will both preserve the core values and mission *and* stimulate progress (perhaps better called missional effectiveness). The core mission will provide continuity and stability, whereas the drive for missional effectiveness will call for continual change and innovation—new direction, new methods, new strategies, and more. Well-articulated mission, vision, and core value statements can help people within the organization see what they are to be and do, but without organization, you simply will not live into your potential.

A teleological organizational system is needed. Our structure must move us into the desired result. For example, if our mission is to *join God's mission to share the kingdom of Christ with all people,* then a structure should be established that will produce those results if it is followed.

Where do we see the emphasis on organization in the Bible? I begin where the Bible begins: "In the beginning God created the heavens and the earth. Now the earth was formless and empty, darkness was over the surface of the deep, and the Spirit of God was hovering over the waters. And God said . . ." (Genesis 1:1–3a, NIV). In the beginning was something we call "chaos." In fact, we really didn't know what to call it because *it* was not a thing—it was nothingness, void, emptiness. To name it is to make it something, but it was nothing. That's why our language fails us in the doctrine of *creatio ex nihilo* ("creation from nothing"). Into the chaos, God spoke, and the result is what we call "the created *order.*"

139

Look at Genesis 1:2 again: "Now the earth was form-less [*tohu*] and empty [*bohu*], darkness was over the surface of the deep, and the Spirit of God was hovering over the waters" (NIV). God created the world using organization. In Genesis 1, God is taking *tohu wabohu* (formlessness and emptiness) and *rightly ordering* it.

God separated things into categories, places, priorities, and times in an order of activity, based on organizational logic. He categorized and delineated light from dark, heavens from earth, land from sea, vegetation and trees, sun, moon, and stars, birds, fish, animals, crawling things, male from female. God created the context that we call "creation" through an organized and organizational process and then put his supreme creation—his divine image—in the middle of this context of created order. It is as if God put his image in the middle of his temple.

W. H. Griffith Thomas writes that "the adjectives 'form-less' and 'empty' seem to be the key to the literary structure of the chapter. The record of the first three days refers to the heaven and earth receiving their 'form,' and the record of the last three days to the filling-up of their 'emptiness.'"[6] Organization is the way God overcame *tohu wabohu*—what we commonly call chaos. Some people disregard organization in favor of organic. However, the opposite of organizational systems is not organic but *chaos*. Organic is in and of itself an organized system. It seems as though the very purpose of creation was to provide an organized context for communion between the triune God and all creation, par-

---

6. W. H. Griffith Thomas, *Genesis: A Devotional Commentary* (Grand Rapids: Eerdmans, 1946), 29.

ticularly humanity. God created everything utilizing principles of *organization*. Organization matters! In fact, all throughout the story of God and his people—throughout the Bible—there is organization. It matters:

- Joseph organized Egypt and saved the nation—and the people of God—from destruction
- The organization of the tribes of Israel, the exit from Egypt, the tabernacle, the priesthood
- The organization contained in the ethical law, setting boundaries for how the people of God should live
- The organization of the Old Testament hymnal, the book of Psalms
- The organization of the Bible itself
- The Proverbs 31 woman is applauded for her organizational skills
- The famous "there's a time for everything" passage in Ecclesiastes 3 can be viewed through the lens of organization
- One of the first threats to *shalom* that arose in the early church following Pentecost was an organizational problem (see Acts 6:1–2); this missional problem was solved through organization
- Paul's letters reflect the need for organization; in his first letter to the Corinthians he says about the act of worship that "all things should be done decently and in order" (14:40), an admonishment that can be extrapolated to include all matters of church life
- Ephesians 4 gives insight on a church organizational rubric
- Instruction for church leaders in 1 Timothy 3 reflects an emphasis on organization

- Even the book of Revelation contains order—the letters were on an organized mail route, and the holy city is very organized

Organization makes something useful, purposeful, intentional, productive, and missional. It maximizes opportunities and resources.

Could it be that the opposite of organization is indeed sin—*tohu wabohu*? For further thinking on this issue, research the prophets and their use *of tohu wabohu.*

Organization should be taken seriously because the opposite of organization is chaos, and chaos opposes the purposes of God. Organization is key to overcoming missional dysfunction.

APPENDIX D

■———————■

Missional Ministry Grid
(Chapters 7 and 10)

	Evangelism	Worship	Discipleship	Compassion	Community Life	Global Missions
Children						
Youth						
University						
Adult						
Senior Adult						
Family						
Missions						
Small Groups						
Men						
Women						
Administration						
Personnel & Parish		Stewardship & Finance		Buildings & Grounds		Special Task Forces

The way this system is designed to function requires each subculture (demographic group within the church) to form a leadership team. I have called these ministry action teams (MATs). The key is for each team to ask the right questions. Asking the right questions will allow the church to minister to the community and culture in which it finds itself. It also allows for the Word to become flesh and live in the midst of the community.

The answers to the questions will differ for each team and each church depending on culture and context, and the questions themselves will be different from team to team, but the approach is the same: ask the questions to generate an appropriate strategy that will help you achieve your missional goals.

Below are sample questions for a specific children's MAT. These questions are not exhaustive and will most likely lead to other questions. They are provided to give you an idea of the framework.

Questions a Children's MAT Might Want to Ask

- What are the most effective ways to evangelize our children?
  - How can we present to our children the opportunity to surrender their lives to Jesus?
- What are the most effective ways to engage our children in authentic worship?
  - What are we doing currently?
    - Is it effective?
  - What else can we do?
    - What should it look like?
- What are the most effective ways to disciple our children?
  - What technology is available?
  - How can we utilize curriculum?
- How can we most effectively engage our children in compassionate ministry?
  - What can we do to lead them into caring for the poor, the hurting, the broken, and the vulnerable in our community?
- What are the most effective ways to build community among our children and their families?

○ How can we create and promote fellowship and care for others in the body of Christ?

• How can we lead our children into a global perspective in relation to the gospel?

○ How can we provide opportunities for our children to engage in advancing the kingdom of Christ globally?

APPENDIX E

■——■

Missional Ministry Pyramid
(Chapter 8)

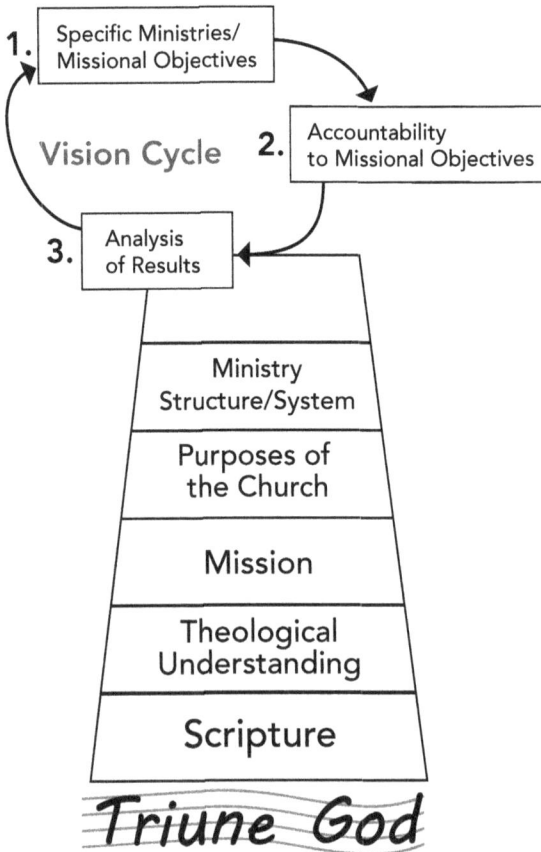

1. Specific Ministries/
   Missional Objectives

Vision Cycle

2. Accountability
   to Missional Objectives

3. Analysis
   of Results

Ministry
Structure/System

Purposes of
the Church

Mission

Theological
Understanding

Scripture

Triune God

APPENDIX F

■——■

Close Your Eyes and See: Transforming Vision into Reality (Chapter 8)

Step 1

Close your eyes and imagine what the church would look like if the church were truly engaged in the mission of God in the world. What do you see?

- What do you see the church doing with the poor around you?
- What do you see the church doing in the places of pain and brokenness around you?
- What do you see the church doing in the communities around you?
- How is the church interacting with people around you?
- What do worship gatherings look like?
  - What do they sound like?
- What methods of discipleship are being utilized?
  - Small Groups?
  - Times for discipleship?
  - Places for discipleship?
- How do you see the church engaged in global missions?

- Teams going to other cultures and alleviating needs, sharing the gospel, being Jesus to others?
- How do you see people entering a faith relationship with Jesus?
  - What does their path look like?
- What does the church look like as it shares life together?
  - Praying together?
  - Caring for one another?

Step 2

Open your eyes and get a view of present reality. Compare what you saw with your eyes closed to what you see with your eyes open. Identify the differences between what is desired and what is currently happening.

Step 3

Prioritize the areas that need attention. The world was not spoken into existence in a single day. Set priorities for the focus of attention and resources.

Step 4

Determine the action plan for addressing the identified areas, starting with top priority. This gets very practical.

- What needs to be purchased?
- What materials need to be created?
- What needs to be developed?
- What dates become important?
- What personnel need to be hired or recruited?

APPENDIX G

■———■

Action Plan for Local Innovation (Chapter 9)

1. Informational Constituency Presentation
Gather together the congregation, the church board/council, or whatever organization is responsible for leading change and discuss the changes that need to occur.

- Address the churchmanship issue. (We should be committed to the church regardless of whether our opinions are chosen. This issue is not worth leaving your church over.) The goal is to help the congregation be truly committed to the local church itself before any decisions concerning change are made. This approach can produce an atmosphere of trust. Only in an atmosphere of trust can any issue be honestly explored and discussed.

- Present the rationale for the proposed change. Use visuals if appropriate. Let them see what the change would look like.

- Imagine together what the future might be like if the change does not occur. What is the cost of not changing?

- Ask people who would like to respond to the issue to do so in writing (both those in favor and those who oppose). Parameters for responding should be given (1 page, typed, address the issues, no personal attacks, no anonymous responses, etc.).

2. Responses Considered

The task force gathers the responses and presents them to the team charged with making the decision. Dialogue about the responses.

o Which ones are informative?

o Which ones are emotional but irrational?

o What changes need to be made to the change proposal to make it better?

o What issues need to be addressed with the congregation in light of the responses?

3. Second Congregational Presentation

• Let them know the team has reviewed and considered the responses.

• Address the pertinent issues raised and remind them of the cost of not changing.

• Inform them of changes to the proposal and of what the final proposal is.

• If the situation is tense and has the potential to be explosive, use a point/counterpoint format of presenting the written objections and the written responses.

• Address any issues that may have been overlooked earlier.

4. Sunday Straw Pole/Survey:

Distribute a survey (whether to use an electronic or hard-copy method is up to you) giving a wide range of responses about the change for the general congregation to weigh in.

☐ I am in total agreement with the proposed change.

☐ I believe the proposed change to be a fairly good idea.

☐ It doesn't matter to me.

☐ I believe change is needed, but not this particular solution. (My suggestion: _____

_____)

☐ I do not support the proposed change but will support the will of the majority.

☐ I do not support the proposed change and will leave this church if this change is adopted.

5. Decision
The decision is made whether to adopt or reject the change.

6. Assure the Congregation
Publicly commit to reevaluating the change to assess its effectiveness after a specific period of time.

Goals of this Process Include:
- Create a measurable response
- Utilize visuals to help people see the proposed change
- Leave room for various outcomes
- Create a common base of understanding and purpose
- Promote constructive dialogue
- Promote Christian responses

Note: Any denominational governance requirements for change should be respected and followed.

Note: In developing a plan for initiating change, a timeline should also be developed and shared.

APPENDIX H

■———■

Missional Objective Spreadsheets (Chapter 10)

Missional objectives are the answers to the questions asked on the missional ministry grid. For example:

- What is the most effective way to disciple youth in our culture?
- How can we most effectively engage youth in compassionate ministry?
- What is the most effective way to help youth encounter God in worship?
- How do we engage youth in global missions?

When these and other questions are answered, the results can be placed in a chart. It could also be helpful to add two additional columns to the sample: 1) Budget and 2) Notes. This will allow the leadership to see a clearer picture of what is planned for the year.

Managing the process for accountability to missional objectives can be challenging without a system. Without an organized approach to accountability, this entire methodology can degenerate into an exercise in futility. It will become a great discussion with wonderful plans but no follow-through. As the saying goes, it will be a mile wide and an inch deep.

The sample Youth MAT chart presents an example of missional objectives for a particular ministry action team followed by an example of an organizational grid for multiple MATs, arranged in such a way as to be manageable. These samples are not comprehensive and are intended to be examples only. Add MATs as needed. The dates chosen align with a calendar year, although aligning with a fiscal year may be preferred.

Youth MAT

Note: The purpose codes align with the identified purposes on the missional ministry grid (evangelism, worship, discipleship, compassion, community life, and global missions). Your identified purpose codes may be different because your missional ministry grid may be different.

Missional Objective	Purpose (D-E-W-CM-CL-GM)	Date to Begin	Date to Complete	Marketing Dates
Wednesday Night	All	Ongoing		
Sunday SS	D-CL	Ongoing		
Monthly Activity	E-CL	Ongoing		
Denominational Youth Event	D-W-CL	1/17	4/17	1/17
Grad Transition	D-CL	2/17	8/17	4/17
Camp	All	9/16	6/17	3/17
Global Mission Trip	All	6/16	7/17	8/16
Mission Nashville	D-W-CM	9/16	7/17	2/17
6th Grade Transition	D-W-CL	7/17	8/17	7/17
Back to School Gathering	All	7/17	8/17	7/17
Helping with Homeless Ministry	CM	10/17	4/18	10/18
After School Gatherings	D-CL	Ongoing		
Extracurricular Events	CL	Ongoing		
Fall Retreat	D-W-CL	8/17	10/17	8/17
Denominational Youth Event	D-W-CL	4/17	11/17	9/17
Celebrate Year	W-CL	12/17	12/17	12/17
Winter Retreat	D-W-CL-E	9/17	2/18	9/17
Mission Trip to Haiti	All	8/17	7/19	8/17

MAT Missional Objectives Spreadsheet

Note: The pastor can monitor this in a monthly or weekly meeting by asking for a report from each MAT leader. This can even be done via email in contexts with no pastoral staff, although in person is preferred. SD and CD are for "start date" and "completion date."

DATE	CHILDREN MAT	YOUTH MAT	WORSHIP MAT
Ongoing	Weekly Discipleship Weekly Worship Weekly Parent Emails Monthly Communication Monthly MAT Meeting	Midweek Gatherings Weekly Discipleship Weekly Worship Weekly Youth Communication Monthly Parent Communication Afterschool Gatherings Extracurricular Events Monthly MAT Meeting	Weekly Worship Planning Worship Team Rehearsal Worship Band Rehearsal Weekly Prayer Times Resource Children and Youth MATs as needed Monthly MAT Meeting
January	CD: Volunteer Training Communicating the Annual Calendar of Events to Parents SD: Children's Musical/ Drama SD: Easter Planning	CD: Volunteer Training SD: Denominational Youth Event Homeless Ministry	CD: Volunteer Training SD: Rehearsal for Easter Worship Event—Winter Retreat SD: Good Friday Worship Event Planning
February	SD: VBS SD: Camps SD: Catechism Classes SD: Children's Camp Planning	SD: Grad Transition Homeless Ministry CD: Winter Retreat	
March	CD: Preteen Global Mission Event SD: Children's Global Mission Event	SD: Promo for Denominational Youth Camp Homeless Ministry	
April	CD: Children's Musical/Drama CD: Easter Celebration Event CD: Catechism Classes SD: School's Out Party SD: Baby Day SD: Fall Sports League	CD: Denomination Youth Event CD: Homeless Ministry SD: Denominational Fall Event	CD: Good Friday Worship Event CD: Easter Worship Event

May	SD: Volunteer Appreciation Day Planning CD: School's Out Party CD: Baby Day CD: Children's Global Mission Event	SD: Volunteer Appreciation Day Planning CD: School's Out Party	SD: Volunteer Appreciation Day Planning SD: Rehearsal for Fall Worship Event
June	CD: VBS SD: Back to School Party SD: Promo for Denominational Preteen Retreat	CD: Denominational Youth Camp SD: Promo and Planning for Global Mission Trip for Next Year SD: Back to School Party	
July	CD: Children's Camp	CD: Mission Nashville SD: Preteen Transition	
August	CD: Back to School Party CD: Volunteer Appreciation Day	CD: Grad Transition CD: Volunteer Appreciation Day CD: Preteen Transition CD: Back to School Party SD: Fall Retreat SD: Mission Trip to Haiti	
September	SD: Sports League CD: Denominational Preteen Retreat SD: Children's Christmas Musical/ Drama	SD: Denominational Youth Camp Planning for Next Year SD: Promo & Planning for Mission Nashville SD: Winter Retreat	CD: Fall Worship Event SD: Christmas Worship Event—Fall Retreat
October	CD: Calendar of Events CD: Trunk or Treat	SD: Homeless Ministry CD: Fall Retreat SD: Christmas Celebration	
November	SD: Preteen Global Mission Planning	Homeless Ministry CD: Denominational Fall Event	
December	CD: Children's Christmas Musical/ Drama	Homeless Ministry CD: Christmas Celebration	CD: Christmas Worship Event
Beyond	Preteen Mission Trip	Global Mission Trip (July)	
TBD	Parent Class Biannual Parent Meetings Second Volunteer Training	Mission Trip to Haiti Exact Dates	

155

APPENDIX I

■——■

Leadership Response Card
(Chapter 10)

The purpose of a Leadership Response Card is to inform an individual of consideration for a ministry role. It also serves the purpose of communicating expectations. Not all ministry roles rise to the level of such expectations. As explained in chapter 10, the greater the responsibility, the greater the expectation of a leader's character.

This approach assumes the desire for authentic leadership. Because we are joining the *missio Dei*, we must take seriously spiritual leadership development. Remember it is Christology, then missiology, then ecclesiology. The mission of Jesus calls for leadership accountability.

This card can be utilized for those serving in roles of greater responsibility. It is a great opportunity for discussion within a leadership team regarding which ministry roles should receive such expectations. It is also a great opportunity for personal discussion with the one being considered for a ministry role.

Leadership Response Card

The Bible establishes qualifications for all who would serve the body of Christ through spiritual, servant, incarnational leadership. It is therefore necessary for all who serve to agree to the following leadership qualifications. Thank you for prayerfully considering this vital ministry.

Please check the following where appropriate:

_____ I am in right relationship with God.

_____ I am in agreement with the theology of this church.

_____ I am committed to the mission and vision of this church.

_____ I faithfully tithe at least 10% of my income through this church.

_____ I am currently involved in ministry to the church in the following capacities:

_____

_____

_____ I faithfully attend this church.

_____ I am seeking to be a person of integrity and Christlike character.

_____ I am willing to be part of the team to help accomplish God's purposes for this church. If for any reason I find myself out of alignment with any of the above, I will voluntarily resign my ministry position.

_____ I willingly accept this responsibility   _____ I respectfully decline at this time

Signature: _____ Date: _____

APPENDIX J

——■

Leadership Development Retreat Plan

It is good, periodically, for leadership teams to bond and plan together over periods of concentrated time, such as during a dedicated weekend retreat. What follows is a suggested plan for such a weekend. It is meant to be flexible and suggestive, not comprehensive or rigidly fixed. You may find it helpful to distribute copies of this very book (*From the Ground Up*) and ask all attenders to read it in preparation for the discussions occurring at this retreat.

First, you'll need to create a team to plan and organize the weekend, covering issues including:

- Discuss and clarify goals for the weekend.
- Ask and answer: What needs to be accomplished during this time?
- Determine the specifics of the schedule.
- Make arrangements for refreshments.
- Decide locations for breakout sessions.
- Prepare for technological needs (sound, visuals, etc.).
- Identify all the questions for each particular MAT and distribute those questions to each MAT leader in advance of the weekend.

The following schedule is designed for a Friday night through Saturday noon. It could also be accomplished in a variety of other time frames, depending on your context and specific needs and availability.

Friday Night (2 hours)

Welcome (5 minutes)

Session 1 (15 minutes)
*Purpose and plan for the weekend
*Prayer time

Session 2 (45 Minutes)
*Overview of local church/organization
*Presentation of missional ministry grid specifically tailored to your context
*Present the questions for each MAT to discuss

Session 3 (30 Minutes)
*Create space for each MAT to meet and ask any questions regarding their mission, their role on the MAT, and goals for the weekend. This can be done in a large gathering place (such as a gym) around tables.

Note: In most churches there will be people involved in multiple MATs. This is common but not necessarily ideal. Although it may be necessary to have people in multiple roles, the leader needs to assist them toward where they want to concentrate their leadership efforts.

Session 4 (30 Minutes)
*Q&A
*Devotional thought on the need for volunteer accountability (willingness of spiritual leaders to be held accountable regarding character, commitment, and completion of goals)

Saturday Morning (3 Hours)

Welcome (5 Minutes)

Session 1 (20 Minutes)
*Leadership teaching on vision, leadership character, joining the mission of God, or any other appropriate topic
*Prayer

Session 2 (1.5–2 Hours)
*Break out into MATs for the purpose of creating a plan of ministry for the year by answering the questions raised for MATs in the missional ministry grid. The MAT leaders can lead their MAT into answering the questions, giving both start dates and completion dates, and spend time on particular budgeting issues.
*Each MAT should determine when it will meet monthly to analyze previous activities and events regarding missional effectiveness, monitor the status of current goals, and look ahead to upcoming months. Monthly meetings can occur by videoconferencing if that's more convenient.

Session 3 (30 Minutes)
*Plenary session in which MATs can share one item each from their ministry planning time
*Prayer